THE ISSUES
WE FACE
...and Some Biblical Answers

Family of Faith Library

THE ISSUES WE FACE

...and Some Biblical Answers

Bill Stephens
Compiler

BROADMAN PRESS
Nashville, Tennessee

© Copyright 1974 · Broadman Press

All rights reserved

4282–30

ISBN: 0–8054–8230–x

Library of Congress Catalog Card Number: 73–85702

Dewey Decimal Classification: 261.8

Printed in the United States of America

Each chapter except "Sex: A Christian View" is reprinted by permission from *People* magazine, published by The Sunday School Board of the Southern Baptist Convention.

Contents

Contributors

D. P. Brooks is editor of *Advanced Bible Study and Young Adult Bible Study,* at the Sunday School Board of the Southern Baptist Convention, and is author of *The Bible: How to Understand and Teach It* (Broadman Press).

Dr. Robert Dean is editor of *Adult Bible Teacher,* at the Sunday School Board of the Southern Baptist Convention, and is author of *First Corinthians for Today* (Broadman Press).

Clyde Lee Herring is pastor of Calvary Baptist Church in Garland, Texas. He has written Sunday School curriculum for youth and articles for several Southern Baptist magazines.

William H. Stephens is editor of inspirational books, Broadman Press. He formerly was editor of *People.*

Shirley L. Stephens has written articles and curriculum for a variety of Southern Baptist publications for adult and youth; is author of the booklet, *Teaching Tips for You;* and served a number of months as interim editor of *Context* and *Young Adult Sunday School,* at the Sunday School Board of the Southern Baptist Convention.

Preface

Evangelical Christians hold the key to America's ethical future. That is a brazen statement, admittedly. Evangelicals will not produce the only ethical influences, of course. The influences will range from that of the producers of pornography to the most ethereal scholar. But *influences* in themselves do not determine the outcome. Rather, an unpredictable combination of those influences will result from their digestion within the common experiences of everyday living.

The ordinary people in each of America's cultures—black, white, or otherwise; from low income to high income—determine a nation's culture. For example, sociologists will not determine marriage practices by predicting the future. Marriage practices will be determined by ordinary people, in the main, living out their marriage relationships. These ordinary people comprise a huge mixer that receives raw materials in its spout, churns them up, and finally produces a mix that does not resemble any of the many ingredients that first went in.

Evangelical Christianity has more input into the mixer than any other group in America, and influences more Americans than any other group. Moreover, evangelical Christianity now is experiencing a tremendous thrust of power that promises to leave its mark on America for a long time to come.

This book is by and for evangelicals. The writers are committed to Jesus Christ as Lord and Savior, and each one stands firmly on the Bible, full-faced toward the future. Each chapter was written from that confident stance.

Except for chapter one, previously unpublished, "Sex: A Christian View," each chapter appeared earlier in *People* magazine, as follows: "Dilemma: The Church and the Divorcee" and "A Place for Us," June, 1972; "What About Abortion?" February, 1971; "The Bible and Women's Liberation" (expanded here), September, 1972; the three "The Future" chapters as a series in November, December, and January, 1971–72; "65 Is a Lousy Age," December, 1972; "Mercy Killing: Right or Wrong?" (expanded), February, 1973; "Cremation: Is It Christian?" May, 1973; "Let's Stop Political Pollution!" October, 1972; "A New Case for an Old Conviction," June, 1971.

Each chapter provides a basic introduction to an issue we face, and each one presents some biblical answers, designed to provide evangelical Christians with additional ingredients to pour into that huge mixer.

I

Sex: A Christian View
Bill Stephens

Sex is not something you do; it's what you are.

The rationale for a Christian view of sex is based on that distinction. Sex is both a *composite* of all a person has become throughout his life and a *molder* of what he is becoming. It is because of this total involvement of sex with personhood that the biblical view of sex is valid today.

Sex thought in America today is complex. Every kind of sexual philosophy and practice is represented, from the most bestially dehumanizing to the highest expression of personhood. This diversity has created significant challenges to the Christians who must think through and state a Christian view of sex.

We have two great problems in presenting a case for the biblical view. First, people don't think about sex with great logic. The hormones become involved. Men and women tend to give more credence to arguments that allow free expression of those aroused emotions. Second, during the past several centuries, our stand on sex has been shaped out of the realities of life: the dangers of pregnancy and venereal disease. Building a case against premarital and extramarital sex relations was relatively simple.

Of course, the pill has not solved the pregnancy problem, and certainly not the venereal disease problem, which is near epidemic proportions now. These facts of life are important reasons why sex only within marriage is the Christian ideal, but pregnancy and venereal disease are problems that can and probably will be solved—sooner or later—through technology.

Our easy-to-build case was a curse as well as a blessing. We drifted away from a solidly biblical view of sex. We used arguments that were based on the secular "sex is something you do" syndrome.

SEX IS SOMETHING YOU DO: THE SECULAR VIEW

The secular climate of opinion is that sex is a natural act that has been repressed by moralists. Freedom from moralism, so goes the claim, will eliminate many of the hangups society has developed. *The Sensuous Man, The Sensuous Woman, Portnoy's Complaint, The Happy Hooker,* and a superfluity of other supposedly freed up books do not take sufficient account of the complexities inherent in sex relations.

Playboy magazine, the most significant pioneer and developer of the prevailing climate, has made some effort to deal with these complexities. Editorially, *Playboy* insists that casual sex is dangerous and that sex is for people who care about each other. However, *Playboy* reveals its casualness toward the interrelatedness of sex and personality in several ways: by portraying group sex; by picturing beautiful women erotically; by promoting the most erotic scenes from X- and R-rated movies; by many of its short stories and most of its jokes; and by its insistence that anything is all right as long as no one else is hurt. (The trademark portrayal of beautiful women, incidentally, reveals two serious sexual errors: women are demeaned to the status of objects, and sex is portrayed as the purview of the young and beautiful.)

SEX IS WHAT YOU ARE: THE BIBLICAL VIEW

Ironically, the "free" sex view is neither psychologically nor biblically sound, because sex is what you are. *This Christian view of sex upholds chastity outside of marriage, liberates persons to enjoy sex to the greatest degree within marriage, and establishes a base for men and women not married to one another to love one another on a level of experience that generally has been unknown.*

The questions used to approach the subject of sex usually are the wrong ones. "Why should sex be wrong if you are careful to avoid pregnancy?" and "Why sublimate life's most natural function?" are only two in a long series. But the question that must be explored is: *How is sex related to love, personhood, and the development of a better society?*

Theologians and Bible scholars are familiar with the term "progressive revelation," which means that God revealed himself to man throughout the centuries as man was able to understand. Succeeding periods of Old Testament history see the Hebrew writers proclaiming an ever-higher concept of God and of ethics. Insights regarding sex developed in accordance with progressive revelation.

Beginning with the assertion that all creation is good (Gen. 1), the Old Testament moves to an emphasis on procreation as one of the highest blessings afforded man. Polygamy and the levirate law supported the emphasis on procreation. A double standard existed between men and women: Concubines were common; man's conduct with prostitutes was accepted, while sexual purity among women was strictly enforced (Gen. 38:23; Deut. 22:21; 23:18; Lev. 19:29; 21:9). Even during those early Old Testament days, however, sex between husband and wife was an expression of love and companionship. A newly married man was exempted one year from serving either as a warrior or in a business capacity that would take him away from home, so that he and his bride could enjoy each other (Deut. 24:5). Proverbs 5:18–19 admonishes a man to enjoy sex relations with his wife.

As the years passed, marriage and sex practices were raised to higher levels. Monogamy became the rule and the one man/one woman relationship was highly praised (Prov. 31:10–31). The various prophets presuppose monogamy.

The Song of Solomon was, for several centuries, interpreted as an allegory of the love of God for his people or the love of Christ for the Church. The obvious interpretation, however, is that it is

an ode to the love between a man and a woman. The *Song* portrays
the fidelity of a young woman who refuses the appealing glamour
of a royal court in order to be the wife of a poor shepherd lover.
The *Song* is full of references to the sexual enjoyment the two
lovers share.

The New Testament underscores the view of liberated sex within
marriage (1 Tim. 3:2,12; 5:14; Titus 1:6; 1 Cor. 9:5; Eph. 5:22–33;
Col. 3:18–19; Heb. 13:4; 1 Pet. 3:7). On the other hand, sex relations outside of marriage are strictly prohibited (Matt. 5:27; 14:3,4;
John 4:18; 2 Cor. 12:21; Gal. 5:19,22; Eph. 5:3,5; Col. 3:5; 1 Thess.
4:3; 1 Cor. 6:9–10; and others).

But beyond these statements on sex practices and attitudes, Jesus
added a new dimension of sexual understanding. His "one flesh"
statement (Matt. 19:5–6) referred not so much to physical union
of two bodies, but rather to the total blending in marriage of two
lives into one symphony.

Marriage is a total commitment of one person to another. Sex,
at its best, is a total commitment expression of love. Sex serves as
a bonding influence in marriage because it allows for expression
of the total person—everything about him, even those subconscious traits of which he himself is not aware. Such acquaintance
may create problems between lovers, since they may not be aware
of what they are communicating. Of course, difficult sex relations
may be due to negative sexual preconditioning. But more probably
such difficulties may be a danger signal regarding the whole relationship. In such cases, the total commitment of two lovers within
marriage provides a foundation for them to maintain the marriage
while discovering what the problem is and working it out. The
point is that when a person (or two persons) work out such a
relationship problem they gain insights that make them better
persons and the marriage rises to a new level of love. Outside of
marriage, such incompatibility likely would cause the relationship
to terminate (which otherwise might develop into real love if given
a chance) and whatever caused the incompatibility is *compounded*

rather than *solved*.

SEX IS WHAT YOU ARE: EVIDENCE EXAMINED

Quite a lot of research is available, though not nearly enough, on how various sexual practices affect later life. Unfortunately, psychologists interpret the results in accordance with preconceived ideas. That fact indicates the uncertainty of available evidence. For example, college students often are told that sexual repression brings about serious frustration. The view is not supported by research.

Margaret Mead compared the girls in the Manus tribe, who practice complete sexual repression before marriage, with Samoan girls who are unrestricted sexually.[1] The Manus girls experience no more stress and strain in growing up than do the Samoans.

A number of writers (Erik Erikson, Ira Gordon, Evelyn Duvall, and Peter Bertocci, to name a few) present pretty solid evidence that premarital sexual practice affects every dimension of character: self-esteem, self-respect, self-image, attitudes toward other people, dependability, and so forth. Undoubtedly, many factors other than sex practice enters into the development of character attributes. Nonetheless, the comparisons are significant.

Research indicates that the person who maintains virginity until adulthood better develops the ability to relate to people of both sexes, for he must learn to relate to persons as *persons,* rather than as objects of personal satisfaction. Significantly, early and frequent sexual experimentation appears to lower the chances of sexual fulfillment in marriage.

All through early life, more obviously during adolescence, emotional and mental patterns are set toward sex. Essentially, the same view a person has toward sex *prior* to marriage carries over into marriage. The attitudes one develops toward sex partners cannot be left behind for a different attitude toward a life mate. If sex is practiced prior to marriage as though it is primarily a physical drive to be satisfied, the person will not psychologically relate sex well to love. Sex and love will remain separate even in marriage. In love, sex is related intrinsically to the partner, not to the self. The love kind of sex, then, is by far the best kind of sex. A person must learn to express love *without* sex in order to *unify* love and sex.

The research of Masters and Johnson (they measure physical sexual responses) dominates the field today in research on sex. The team has contributed some important understanding, but their emphasis should not be considered the sum total of what sex is all about. Sex is the great communicator, and communication toward oneness is what sex is all about.

SEX COMMUNICATES

A man and a woman bring to the sex act all they are: childhood impressions, hangups, frustrations, joys, victories, hurts, anger, ecstasy, attitudes toward other people. A person goes to bed with his nose, his funny-shaped knees, his pride, his attitude toward his partner. Sex includes all that happens during the hours before, including screaming bosses and screaming kids. Two people in love communicate all that through the sex act. Little can be hidden. But also communicated—unspoken and perhaps subconscious—are attitudes of dominance, subservience, disregard, acceptance, equality, concern.

When each partner seeks to speak the language of sex with his mate, sex reaches the heights of ecstasy God intended it to reach. A husband who pays attention may discover that he is too dominating, not just in sex but in other areas of marriage. A wife can know when her husband needs an extra dose of sympathy because of his work. Sex on the level of communication becomes a personhood developer, and the marriage itself develops to a oneness that is more profound than the sum total of both personalities.

Sex on the level of communication is threatening, for a person must bare his soul more than his body. He reveals who he is, and the revelation is to himself as well as to his mate. If a man is a male chauvinist, he can discover that through sex. If a woman is docile sexually but otherwise aggressive and cheerful, the contrast should tell her to examine her marriage. Is she being open and honest with her husband? Will he let her be open and honest? Facing up to the problem (whoever is at fault) and working out the difficulty adds new dimensions of strength to the marriage.

Two lovers should be concerned about each other intensely enough to express themselves totally to one another in sex, without pretending, without concern as to who is supposed to be the aggressor. That kind of freedom is sexually charged. Christian sex is better sex because two lovers are liberated toward one another, with the totality of each life committed to the other. Each person in such a relationship instills a feeling of worth in the partner, so that each can develop to his highest potential.

Sex often is not biblical even within marriage, though. A man and wife may have sex relations, but may not be "making love." Sex may be a neutral or even a negative factor in marriage.

That kind of sex is sub-Christian. If a husband uses his wife primarily in sex to satisfy his drive, his view of sex is distinctly sub-Christian. If a wife's sex role simply is "doing her duty," her view of sex is distinctly sub-Christian. Any view of sex that separates the sex act from love is a low view of sex, for the act becomes self-centered or reflects an attitude of martyrdom.

SEX AND THE SINGLE ADULT

Why should a person not enjoy sex just because he chooses to remain single?

An insistence on "sex for the single person" essentially is a denial of personhood for the single person. The view asserts that a person cannot be a person without having sexual relations.

The truth is that the Bible answers the question quite directly: Premarital and extra-marital sexual relations are prohibited. The view, of course, is challenged severely in today's world. Nevertheless, it must stand as the Christian's guideline.

Paul emphasized his preference that Christians remain single. He himself preferred the single life because of his call (1 Cor. 7). In that passage, he advised those who could not contain their sex drives to marry (vv. 2,9). But this often-used passage in which Paul is frequently assailed was written when Paul believed that persecution of Christians was imminent. He knew that persecution would be harder on the married. At the same time, Paul is convinced that the single person can serve God in ways the married cannot. Jesus emphasized the same point (Matt. 19:12).

The central fact in a Christian's mind must be that which Paul emphasized: commitment to Christ, the will of God for his life. This level of discipleship is the same for all, married or not. It is when discipleship is ignored or placed in a secondary position that sex for the single Christian becomes such a thorny philosophical problem.

No Christian is aswim in the sea of mankind. The fact that one is redeemed presupposes that he has a purpose in life. The single person has doors of service open to him that are different (not better nor inferior) from those of the married. Sexual liaisons deter him from discipleship. (Incidentally, sexual temptations probably are not more acute for the single person than for the married, though the temptations may differ. Both the married and the single must contain their sex drives.)

The fact is that full and meaningful lives can be lived without sexual relations. But positively, the biblical view of celibacy for the unmarried presupposes that single adults will live fuller and happier lives without sex, since that sex necessarily does not involve total and permanent commitment.

The allegation just made cannot be proved. Not enough evidence is available to indicate that sexual relations between two unmarried partners who have affection for each other will retard personality development. The subject is too complicated, and society (including researchers) is too unsophisticated to determine the effects of sexual activity on the person. The Christian has to take the biblical view on faith.

The basis of faith, of course, is that God knows more about humanity than we do. Our ignorance is the reason we need a guide. In the face of uncertainty (which works both ways, remember) of the results of sexual relations, the Christian chooses to consider the biblical guidelines as valid because God is not uncertain.

SEX IS WHAT YOU ARE: A CHRISTIAN VIEW OF SEX

The "sex is what you are" view requires the acceptance of persons as persons. The Christian view of sex proclaims that sex is inhibitive and exploitative unless through it persons can express themselves fully and in commitment to a permanent partner.

This view of sex, then, insists that friendship between a man and a woman (single or married to another person) can blossom into beauty best if the two do not become enmeshed in the intrigues of sex. The ability of men and women to form such lasting friendships is closely related to full equality of persons. When this level is reached in society, women naturally can assume their roles alongside men, the necessity of acting out male/female conquest roles no longer a problem. Men and women then can behave warmly toward one another, openly, sincerely, without the threat of sexual liaison hanging over their heads.

Only now are men and women becoming able to relate to one another in a way that is not sexually aggressive. A few years ago a man hardly dared call on a woman in her home, even for business reasons, without taking someone along to forestall gossip. Most pastors left their doors cracked open a bit when counseling with women, so that dutiful secretaries could eliminate criticism. Men and women were sexual antagonists—the conqueror and the conquerable—not *persons* to one another. Even among those who had no conscious sexual goals toward a person, each had to act as though a sexual liaison was a distinct possibility.

Research has left no doubt that a person's sexual behavior is directly related to his self-image. A person's sexual maturity is in direct proportion to his maturity in all of life. When a person develops self-confidence, then, the need diminishes for him to do sexual love dances (much of which is subconscious) every time he is alone with a woman; and women will cease to consider all men as potential sexual aggressors.

To assume that sexual temptation one day will be nonexistent is naive, of course. Any relationship between a man and a woman is sexual in the sense that each is aware of the sexuality of the other, and the awareness makes a difference in the relationship. Nonetheless, a mature Christian sexual standard both allows for such friendships and disallows exploitation.

The ability of a man and a woman to develop a friendship that does not exploit one another sexually is based on the biblical one flesh concept—total commitment of one man and one woman each to the other. A sexual liaison with another person dilutes the commitment to the mate, and at the same time cannot but exploit the persons involved. The creative potentials of sex cannot be experienced. Moreover, sex relations interfere with the development of the friendship. The friendship, when detoured along the sexual route, never can develop as significantly as it otherwise might.

SEX: GOD'S GREAT GIFT

Sex is one of God's greatest gifts to those he created. *One* of God's greatest gifts. A greater gift is individual personhood. Sex is a gift only if it supports that greater gift.

The question, "Why does God allow evil and suffering?" has never been fully answered. Sex, with all of its ramifications, is that kind of question.

In a rather so-so book (*Nun, Witch, Playmate*), theologian Herbert W. Richardson makes a significant statement that celibacy and virginity recur again and again in history immediately after a generation of supposedly liberated people come along to renounce them. (The much lambasted Puritan movement, for example, was a reform against serious sex excesses.) In the book, Richardson presents a novel idea that mankind is evolving sexually. In early history, men and women mimicked animals sexually, the act completely separated from love. But gradually, he believes, sex is being related more and more closely to love. Eventually a man and a woman will not be sexually attracted except to the one person each one loves.

Needless to say, we are light years away from that utopia. But the lesson is well taken, whether the theory is right or wrong. Sex separated from deep love and commitment is inferior sex—physically, emotionally, and spiritually. It is the biblical view of sex that promises a better life.

---

[1] Ruth Strang, *The Adolescent Views Himself* (New York: McGraw-Hill Book Co., Inc., 1957), p. 329.

2

Dilemma: The Church and the Divorcee
Clyde Lee Herring

The nominating committee had filled every vacancy but one. The junior high department still needed a teacher. Sue Barnes was a good choice. She was vivacious. She was a schoolteacher. She was faithful in church. But she was divorced. Should the committee ask her to serve?

This question is faced by multitudes of churches annually. There is important work to be done in the church; there are persons who have the ability to do some of the work, but who cannot because they are divorced. Or can they? That question is the subject of this chapter.

The church must consider three areas to make its decisions: the world in which it functions, the teachings of the Bible, and the will of God for itself and the divorcee.

This is the world the church lives in: The divorce rate is not declining. Though it never has approached the high in America of 610,000 in 1946, the number hovers between 350,000 and 400,000 annually.

With all the apparent unhappiness, one would think Americans would get discouraged with the institution of marriage itself. But Americans seen undaunted. One extensive study (reported in *After Divorce,* by William J. Goode) showed that 94 percent of the women aged thirty and below remarry after divorce. The majority do not wait long to do so. Fifty-four percent of women sampled, aged 20–38, had remarried within twenty-six months after their divorces. Fifty percent of the rest had steady dates. Society has undergone dynamic changes since Goode's book was written, but the principles remain essentially the same.

While some divorced persons repeat marriage failures again and again, many do not.

The incidence of divorce among Christians has risen along with the general rise in divorce in America. The problem became so acute during the '50's and '60's that the Southern Baptist Convention created a Program of Family Ministry to help the churches minister to family life.

Southern Baptist churches in California long have faced the problem of divorce among church members. Though the churches there are theologically conservative, they generally use divorcees in leadership roles. While necessity does not necessarily produce truth, it does propel to action of some kind. The world churches live in today requires some solid thinking and action on the subject.

The only authority Baptists have to determine their faith and practice is the Bible. How does the Bible compel us to act on the subject of divorce and divorcees?

God's original ideal for marriage is clear from the accounts of creation in Genesis: "And the Lord God said, It is not good that the man should be alone; I will make an help meet for him" (Gen. 2:18). After the creation of Eve, the Bible says: "Therefore shall a man leave his father and his mother, and shall cleave unto his wife: and they shall be one flesh" (Gen. 2:24).

The will of God for a man and his wife is that they become "one flesh." The concept is beautifully twentieth century. "Flesh" in this case means the total personhood of the individual.[1] The two persons are intended by God to become one person. This concept and ideal is a treasure of the community of God. His people believe it and strive to realize it. But anyone who has experienced marriage knows that ideals seldom are attained overnight. To expect a man and a woman to become "one flesh" at the moment they are pronounced husband and wife does the concept a terrible injustice. They have only begun the stormy but beautiful journey that hopefully will see two distinct personalities grow to become one.

One key to the current problem is that churches are not adequately sharing the good news—the fantastically good news—about what marriage can become when it is dedicated to God's ideal. Christians often proclaim *survival of marriage* to be the most important goal. Tenure of a marriage is of crucial importance, but tenure does not necessarily encompass quality. And *quality* is of equal importance to the biblical meaning of *one flesh*.

God's one flesh ideal grows out of his love for man. The Genesis 2:18 passage states that Eve was called into existence because Adam needed her. Men and women *need* that which can be experienced only in knowing one another as one flesh: biologically one, sociologically one, and psychologically one. Oneness in such full measure increases the abilities of men and women so they can function more fully as persons.

But what about failure? What does the Bible say about a marriage that is doomed because of human frailty, sin, neglect, misunderstanding, or a bad match of two otherwise good people? The legalists of Jesus' day asked him if it were "lawful for a man to put away his wife for every cause" (Matt. 19:3). Jesus answered by affirming the sanctity of marriage, and he concluded: "Wherefore they are no more twain [two], but one flesh. What therefore God hath joined together, let not man put asunder" (Matt. 19:6).

The Bible view is clear. Marriage failure is a breach of God's ideal; therefore it is wrong. But we are not here discussing the rightness or wrongness of divorce; we are discussing the question of life service for the Christian after divorce. How should he look at himself after divorce and how should the church look at him?

Jesus' contemporaries pressed him further because the law of Moses made provision for divorce (Deut. 24:1–4). Jesus explained why the stopgap law was given: "Moses because of the hardness of your hearts suffered you to put away your wives: but from the beginning it was not so." Jesus insisted on a higher ideal. Does his statement setting forth God's ideal negate the fact that God works through people as they are? Numerous Old Testament examples can be cited to demonstrate that God worked through persons who make mistakes in marriage and sexual relations. But what about such New Testament examples?

When Paul defined the qualities necessary for ministers and deacons, he spoke of their home lives: "A bishop then must be blameless, the husband of one wife . . ." (1 Tim. 3:2); "And let these also first be provided; then let them use the office of a deacon, being found blameless . . . Let the deacons be the husbands of one wife, ruling their children and their own houses well" (vv. 10, 12).

The final word on the meaning of "husband of one wife" has not been written. Dr. E. Glenn Hinson reflects the view of many New Testament scholars with his statement in *The Broadman Bible Commentary:* "Exactly what *the husband of one wife* means here will remain in dispute. Five interpretations have been suggested." Dr. Hinson lists those interpretations. He concludes that: "The general nature of the instructions would probably make the first [faithful to his one wife] or the second [married to one wife at a time, i.e., monogamous] view the most likely."

Whichever view is correct, it is significant that the New Testament does not apply such criteria to any other church office, though several passages include lists of offices.

Paul, after calling for every effort to sustain a marriage in which one partner is a Christian and one is not, concluded that the Christian is "not under bondage" when the marriage is dissolved (1 Cor. 7:10–16). The chapter challenges Christians to keep their commitment to Christ first, whatever their present condition of life.

The principle emerges: Taking the present conditions of life, a Christian still should serve Christ to the best of his ability. Evidently, then, God still works with people as they are, even though he insists that his ideal is not lowered in the process.

The first two areas of investigation (the world the church lives in and the biblical teachings) coalesce into a view of God's people as a fellowship of sinners. Christians are people whose sins are paid for, but who nevertheless still are sinners. Even Paul agonized: "For what I would, that do I not; but what I hate, that do I" (Rom. 7:15).

Jesus makes two pretty important points through the experience of the woman taken in adultery (John 8:1–10). First, his stand was not based on the woman's innocence (she was not), but on the lack of innocence of the crowd. They had no right to condemn, for they were sinners, too, though guilty of sins different from hers. Second, he upheld God's ideal while treating the woman with compassion.

Another point is relevant: Most Christian divorcees are not guilty of low morals like the woman taken in adultery. Though Christians have no right to judge anyone, even the most sinful, how much less do they have a right to relate disdainfully to one whose morals are on a par with their own.

Another principle emerges: Christians *all*—divorced or not—are sinners who must relate to one another equally as sinners. The divorcee has not sinned more, only differently. Christians work together as sinners, each one guilty and forgiven by God, each one with high potential to serve Christ in spite of the problems of the past. If ever a society existed on the fact of the earth that could provide an environment where a divorcee could put life together again, it is the church. Gossips, alcoholics, drug addicts, thieves, uncompassionate persons, and just plain old everyday sinners come to know Christ—or rediscover him—and join together in a church to rebuild their lives.

It is that arena of life-building that is the third area of consideration: the will of God. Consideration for this area must be built on the previous discussion. But ultimately the question must be asked by the divorcee: What is God's will for my life?

God is a top notch personnel director. He does not waste or disregard the talents of his people. And he wants to use those people and talents to the best advantage of his work. The divorcee, then, must prayerfully ask himself what God's will is for his life. His church has the obligation to help him find God's will. The church ought to draw lines only where it is convinced without question that God draws those lines. If any question exists at all, the church should prayerfully consider each case on its individual merits.

With this information in hand, the nominating committee must decide what to do with Sue Barnes. They have at least four alternatives: (1) They may deny her the right to hold any office at all. (2) They may evaluate Sue's qualifications and current relationship to God and enlist her to hold any position she qualified for. (3) They may consider Sue for some offices, but not other ones. (Sue may teach Preschoolers, but not Youth. She may play the piano, but she may not lead a choir.) (4) Similar to number (2), the committee may consider all of Sue's qualifications, but consider the fact that her divorce is one factor that the community will react to positively or negatively.

In their decision, the committee must consider how Sue's service will affect the community. However, the church's witness is another dilemma itself, for the church projects a witness to the community either way it decides. Will the community interpret Sue's place in the church to mean that the church has weakened its stand against divorce? Or if the community learns that Sue cannot serve because she is divorced, will the church be considered legalistic and unloving? Then, too, how will the committee's action affect Sue and her life of service? And how will their action affect the life of the church? Will the church members lower their personal standards, or will they become more redemptive?

Those are good questions. What if Sue were in your church? What would be your decision?

---

[1] T. B. Maston, *The Christian, The Church, and Contemporary Problems* (Waco, Texas: Word, 1968), p. 98.

3

A Place for Us
Shirley Stephens

How do divorced Christians feel about churches? How do they think churches feel about them?

Considerable material is available on what the Bible says about marriage and divorce. The shelves are pretty bare, though, of material on how divorced Christians should relate to Christ's work after divorce.

I interviewed a number of divorcees to discover their feelings. This chapter is the result of that research—not what other people say about their feelings, but what divorced Christians say and feel about themselves and their relationships to their churches. Meet the people I interviewed.

• Jo Ellen's father is a deacon. For as long as she can remember, she has been active in church. She still is, even though she feels a bit out of place. Three years ago, she was divorced.

Nobody in church does or says anything to make Jo Ellen feel unwelcome. Maybe that's the problem—the church doesn't do anything. "For the most part," Jo Ellen asserted, "the church acts as if divorcees do not exist. Ignore them, and they'll go away," she added, only half joking.

• "I blamed God a little bit," Candy admitted when we discussed the breakup of their marriage of thirteen years. "I felt that I had done my best, and yet this happened." When Candy became legally separated, she did not go back to the church where she had been a member. She was ashamed, and she did not want sympathy. Too well, she remembered whispered remarks overheard in her youth,

"She's divorced." Candy moved to another city.

• After fifteen years of marriage, divorce interrupted Bettie's life. For some time she would not teach a Sunday School class on a regular basis as she had done in the past. She was concerned that parents would object, and she was afraid that she would present a poor example to the children. Her feelings persisted even though she believes she had biblical grounds for divorce.

After two years, Bettie and Cliff, who was also divorced, were married. Cliff had not felt guilty, but he was conscious of the thoughts of other people about divorce.

• "I felt divorce was a blot on me," Gay said. Abandoned by her husband, she went from another state back to her home church, though it was to face old acquaintances. She felt like a complete failure. Strongly opposed to divorce, she had, at the age of twenty-two, resigned herself to living separated (without divorce) from her husband for the rest of her life and rearing her child alone. She joined the church choir but would not sing a solo. She did not think people would accept her singing as sincere.

Counseling sessions with her pastor helped Gay realize that she and her son had a future. She met and married Ed, an ordained minister, who also was divorced. Ed was convinced that the marriage of an ordained minister to fail was worse than such failure for anyone else. He is sure that his divorce ended his preaching career. He is a little bitter.

All these persons are committed Christians. They need and want to find their places within a church fellowship. For those who are remarried, many of the problems peculiar to the divorcee are lessened. Acceptance for them is easier. But those who are divorced must continue to live with the frustration of finding—or making—a place for themselves.

I have interviewed these people to discover, firsthand, how they felt or now feel about their divorced status in relationship to God, their respective churches, and Christian people. They were quite willing to share their feelings and frustrations. The opening remarks and impressions are based on responses to the question, **"What were your first thoughts about your relationship to your church after divorce or separation?"** The next question was, **Do you feel accepted by God?**

JO ELLEN: Yes, because I felt that I had done the best I could to save the marriage. Still, I knew that I had fallen short of the ideal. The Bible doesn't justify divorce at all.

BETTIE: It took about a year for me to feel forgiven and accepted by God. I had the nagging feeling that maybe I hadn't done all I could to save the marriage. Yet, I knew I had.

CLIFF: I felt forgiveness from the first. I was determined to straighten out my life.

CANDY: I didn't feel there was anything for God to forgive me for. I had done my best to save the marriage, and my grounds for divorce are biblical.

GAY: Yes. There was never any doubt. But I didn't feel that I deserved a second chance.

What about remarriage?

CANDY: Definitely yes. I will marry again. I am obligated to show that I am not bitter toward marriage. I know it is a beautiful thing—ordained of God. It can be good.

I probably will face some difficulty in finding a preacher to perform the ceremony. Yet, I feel sorry for a preacher who will not marry a divorced person under any conditions. He hasn't interpreted the Bible correctly. He is behind times and too strict if he won't consider the situation. I *expect* to be talked to—I did that before I married the first time. Preachers who think independently would perform the ceremony. I definitely want to be married in church.

ED: I was afraid others would not accept remarriage. When a preacher will not perform the ceremony, I think it indicates his congregation would object.

BETTIE: I had second thoughts about remarriage. I was scared I would make another mistake. Also, I felt a little guilty. Now, when I see how much better off my children are, I wonder why I ever worried.

JO ELLEN: Yes, if the right man comes along. The next time, I'm going to be more careful. I won't settle for anything less than a God-fearing, churchgoing person. I don't think my pastor will perform the ceremony.

GAY: After I decided divorce was the only alternative, I was convinced I could never go back to single life. I simply could not live alone. And, my son needed a father.

How were your relationships with other people affected?

ED: People usually have one of three reactions: project an attitude of rejection, appear stunned, or are helpless. Friends seemed to find it difficult to know how to relate to me—what to talk about, how to act. A divorced person really has to make a new set of friends.

GAY: People whom I really considered friends were very sorry. Others waited to see what would happen.

BETTIE: Sunday School class members were helpful and understanding. They called me up just to talk. I felt they really were concerned. There was never any criticism. Some even offered to keep the children if I wanted to go somewhere.

CLIFF: I don't think many in my Sunday School class knew I was divorced. I experienced no criticism. In fact, I felt that I had more and more friends.

CANDY: When I told my single adult group at church that I was divorced, they were really shocked.

JO ELLEN: I have felt no bad feelings toward me at all—just shock when someone discovers I am divorced. At first, I felt that people were more interested in the dirty details of the divorce rather than really wanting to help me.

Since my husband never went to church with me, it was a while before everyone knew about the divorce. I play the organ in church and have continued to play it since my divorce. No one has said anything to suggest that I quit.

What have been the biggest problems in your church adjustment?

GAY: My biggest problem was trying to find my place—just where I fit in. I had great needs. It was hard to find people to talk to who would understand.

Really turning to God with my problems was also very hard. It is easy to say one should turn to God; it is another matter really to turn to him and talk with him in a time of such deep distress.

ED: Like Gay, trying to find my place was a problem. I needed to find out where the church stands on divorce. When a person has heard all his life that divorce is wrong, he doesn't know what to do when he is divorced. He asks himself the question,"Is the church going to reject me?" The first reaction is defensive—"I'll reject the church."

CANDY: A feeling of aloneness is one of my biggest problems. Everything about society and the church is family. The divorcee is left out.

Finding help for my great needs is another problem. If there is no single adult group for me in a church, I have to work. I definitely feel out of place with a married group. Working drains me if I have no group of my own to provide spiritual strength.

CLIFF: Church Training was my biggest problem. I was always the odd person among couples. I did go to the parties, but I felt out of place. All the games would be for husbands and wives. I guess if I had been with the group ten years I might have gotten used to them, and they might have gotten used to me.

BETTIE: I didn't have any really big problems. I didn't feel left out at parties, because people made an extra effort to make me feel welcome.

JO ELLEN: The problems have been mostly because of my own feelings. I just feel out of place wherever I go. I'm pretty comfortable in Sunday School and Church Training most of the time. When divorce was to be discussed in Church Training, I told the group I was staying home so that they wouldn't have to worry about me.

As far as social life, the church has nothing to offer the divorcee. Everything about the church is built around the family. I feel uncomfortable when I go to a social for couples, even when some women come without their husbands.

Where do you feel you can serve in church?

CANDY: Any place—as far as I feel qualified. However, I am conscious of the possibility that others will object. But I have no qualms about serving anywhere. I have no apologies to make.

BETTIE: I didn't teach before remarriage except for substituting, although I had taught before my divorce. As a divorced person, I hesitated. Now, I feel I could serve in any position I am qualified for.

CLIFF: I feel I could serve any place I am qualified for. I might not have accepted a leadership position while I was divorced, mainly because of the possible objection of parents.

ED: I don't feel others would accept me in a church staff position. I would feel comfortable in any other position in church and with any age group.

GAY: I could serve anywhere I feel qualified for. I am sure of my relationship with God and can defend my position.

JO ELLEN: I definitely feel that I could not teach a Sunday School class. I taught thirteen-year-old girls before my divorce, but I could not do that now. A young girl looks up to her Sunday School teacher. I don't want them to look to me for an example, because it might make them think divorce is all right.

I feel comfortable playing the organ. Leading a choir would be all right, because I wouldn't be teaching subjects which would put me on the spot. I would also be willing to substitute teach.

Do you think churches provide a place for the divorcee?

CANDY: No, but I am willing to make a place.

ED: No. The church is afraid to deal with the problem of divorce.

BETTIE: As far as the children are concerned, they do. But, if a person didn't have children, she would probably feel left out. There is no opportunity to meet others.

JO ELLEN: No.

What can churches do to help the divorcee?

CANDY: A single adult group is a real help. When I had a single adult church group, I sat with them at family night suppers, went on retreats, got together after church. When there is no group in church for me, I have no social life connected with the church. If a person is strengthened by the church, I feel that she can be kept from another marriage failure. She won't be pushed into another mistake.

CLIFF: A single adult group would help eliminate the odd feeling when one is part of a couples' group.

JO ELLEN: I don't necessarily feel that churches should do anything. There is too much danger that they would condone divorce, and that would put marriage on a lower level. I'm not for that.

GAY: Churches should use the talents of divorcees. They should be offered places to serve. Serving others will help ease the pain. To be used restores one's confidence.

Also, the divorcee needs help in adjusting to her status. She needs guidance on such things as how to act on a date. There are rules for the married and single but not for the divorcee. A sharing of what problems to expect and a general orientation to the new status would be helpful. The divorcee should be sought out to help rather than having to ask for help.

ED: Churches need to tackle the problem of divorce. They don't have to say divorce is right, but they should minister to the divorcee. A place should be provided for the divorcee to be with others of his own age and situation, but he should not be segregated into a "class for divorced persons." Divorcees are more comfortable with single adults than with married adults.

Obviously, Christian divorcees have a lot of obstacles to overcome as they relate to their churches. Part of the problem lies in the fact that few churches have a program which includes ministry to divorced persons. Belmont Heights Baptist Church, Nashville, is an exception. This church has a Single Adult department which is composed of single adults and divorced persons. Ed, Gay, and Candy were formerly members of that group. Of the group, Candy said, "When you have a group, you have everything." Through the group, she found the Christian fellowship she so desperately needed in her early period of adjustment. Gay doesn't know what she would have done without the group.

In addition to the single adult group, Ken Trinkle, now working with Florida Southern Baptists in Church Training, recommends a short-term discussion group for divorced persons. The goals for such a group might be:

1. To provide an opportunity to discuss mutual problems and concerns;

2. To reach some persons with Christian concern who may never otherwise be part of any church activity;

3. To demonstrate that the church does care about the hurts and struggles of persons who have experienced the trauma of divorce;

4. To allow persons who have been hurt to express themselves in a congenial and sympathetic setting;

5. To strengthen the family life of those who participate;

6. To assist in restoring faith in themselves, in Christ, and in others;

7. To discover, through individual and group reactions, what other needs can be met by a concerned church, and possible attitudes and ideas which need to be changed concerning this ever increasing group in our society today.

Belmont Heights has shown that churches are not afraid to tackle the divorce problem. Yet, if every church had a similar program, divorcees still would have problems of adjustment. Another aspect of the divorcees' problem rests in their inability to accept themselves.

In many instances, divorcees' own strong feelings about divorce create personal feelings of guilt that are hard to eradicate. Jo Ellen is convinced that there is no justification for divorce. Yet, she wants to remarry and make a new life for herself and her two children. Gay did not feel she deserved a second chance. At the same time, she knew she could not live alone for the rest of her life. Even though Bettie believed she had biblical grounds for divorce, she still felt guilty. Actually, the problem is twofold: Both the church and the divorcee reflect attitudes of unacceptance.

Several of the divorcees interviewed admittedly expected the worst from other Christians."I didn't give people credit for being understanding," Ed said. Yet, he did find many people understanding and helpful. He was sure others would not accept his remarrying, but they have. Jo Ellen stated that the problems have been mostly because of her own feelings rather than the actions of others. And it is possible that people would have been understanding if Candy had gone back to the church where she was a member. She simply did not give them a chance—even though she feels that the church has loosened up a lot in regard to divorce, especially when someone is living in a destroying situation. It is also possible that Bettie and Cliff would have experienced no criticism if they had taken regular teaching positions before remarriage.

Churches are composed of people who hold various attitudes ranging from a deep desire to accept Christian divorcees as the fellow-Christians they are, to those who believe that any effort at acceptance implies a lower view of marriage. Nevertheless, divorcees should give Christians a chance to demonstrate acceptance. An "I know you won't accept me attitude" will run off even the most well-intentioned.

So, like many problems, there are two sides. On the one hand, divorcees must not live in the shadow of the past. On the other hand, most churches have exerted little or no effort to provide places for divorcees. They must accept the fact that divorce happens to committed Christians and make plans to minister to divorced persons.

4

What About Abortion?
Bill Stephens

The Supreme Court in early 1973 ruled that during the early weeks of pregnancy abortion is a decision to be made by a woman and her doctor. For good or ill, the decision shifted the burden of responsibility for abortion to the individual conscience.

Since a biblical and moral argument can be made both for and against abortion, this chapter is arranged as a debate. Arguments supporting both views have been gathered and arranged in a fashion that hopefully is not biased, so that the reader can reach his own conclusion. The arguments begin with the direct biblical material, then continue through every argument this writer could find on either side of the issue.

Is there some way either of you can support your arguments from Scripture?

PRO

Not directly. Exodus 21:22–24, though, reads: "If men strive, and hurt a woman with child, so that her fruit depart from her, and yet no mischief follow: he shall be surely punished, according as the woman's husband will lay upon him; and he shall pay as the judges determine. And if any mischief follow, then thou shalt give life for life, eye for eye, tooth for tooth, hand for hand, foot for foot, burning for burning, wound for wound, stripe for stripe."

The implication is that the fetus is not a human being in the sense that the woman is. Whatever injury *she* sustains is to be exacted in kind from the one who injured her. But if the fetus is so injured as to cause a miscarriage, some agreed-upon monetary payment is all that is required.

CON

Since there is no direct biblical teaching on abortion, we must look to the customs of that day. An Assyrian law dated between 1450 and 1250 B.C. demanded death by torture in cases of abortion. The law of Moses called for more severe penalties in matters of sexual misconduct than did the laws of Israel's neighbours. We can assume, then, that abortion was considered murder by Israel. If it were different from surrounding cultures, some law would have spelled out the difference. In regard to my friend's citing of the miscarriage passage, I must point out that there is a distinctive difference between the planned taking of a fetus and an accidental miscarriage. Probably, the law recognized that what was done was done, and was not intentional in the first place.

Additionally, the Old Testament indicates that God was active in conception (Gen. 29:31; 30:22; Ruth 4:13, etc.) and in the development of the fetus (Ps. 139:13–18 and others). So to take the life of a fetus is God's decision alone. God told Jeremiah that he had his hand on him before he was conceived. What if Jeremiah had been taken by abortion?

PRO

The same passage points out that if a man accidentally kills another man, he must flee to a city of refuge to avoid being killed in return. If causing a miscarriage is as serious an offense as accidentally killing a man, why was not the offender required to flee to a city of refuge?

In regard to Jeremiah being lost to history because of abortion, I must point out that his parents, like Christian parents today, would seek God's will in having children. Since Jeremiah was raised in a God-fearing home, he would not have been lost to history.

CON

Anger resulting in acts of hostility needed to be restrained. Consequently, the law provided for that restraint. In the case of an unborn child, such hostility is not normally a factor. A man would have no reason to flee. Hence the difference in laws.

What about the historical position of churches and theologians of the past? Can we learn anything from them on this subject?

PRO

As a matter of fact, opinion was divided for centuries. Tertullian, about A.D. 240, said that abortion was murder only after the fetus had reached the point in its development when it became human. St. Augustine, in the early fifth century, distinguished between the living and the not-yet-living fetus. Eventually, the debate centered around the question of when the soul entered the body, a question impossible to determine. Even Karl Barth, as dogmatic as he was against abortion, allowed for it when the mother's life was in danger.

CON

The earliest teaching on abortion we know of is recorded in the *Didache* (the Teaching of the Twelve Apostles), written between A.D. 120 and 160. The *Didache* had wide circulation in the early church and was almost included in the New Testament. It says, "And this is the second commandment of the teaching. Thou shalt do no murder . . . Thou shalt not murder a child by abortion. . . ." There is some question about Tertullian's belief, too. He inferred that the start of man's physical and spiritual natures coincided. And Augustine, along with others, was reluctant to say when the soul enters the body. Then, finally, Pope Sixtus V, in 1588, ended the argument in the Roman Church by stating that all abortions at any period of development were murder.

PRO

Nevertheless, that argument by the Pope was not accepted in England. They did not consider abortion a criminal offense until the fetus began movement. And I might also note that however influential the *Didache* was in the early church, it did *not* make it into the New Testament.

CON

Regardless of whose argument is better supported by church history, of course, we must remember that the churches made many misjudgments—enough to bring on a Reformation.

PRO

I agree. But I must also point out that civil law has been heavily influenced by church law. Laws in England, from which we derived our own laws, were passed against abortion because of the danger of infection and death to the mother before the days of antiseptics. Now, abortion under hospital conditions is *seven times safer* than childbirth itself. If the reasons for abortion laws have passed, let's repeal the laws.

CON

I don't think an across-the-board repealing of abortion laws will solve anything. Let's revise the laws so that they will require what *should* be required. The reasons for passing abortion laws in the last century are not binding on us now. There are other valid reasons to have abortion laws.

How do you feel about the way religious convictions should influence abortion legislation?

PRO

They should not. To force religious convictions on a nation or state is to deny religious freedom. Every law should allow for as much freedom of viewpoint as possible. One group's religious values should not be impressed on the general population. The abortion decision is between a mother and her doctor. Even many Roman Catholic spokesmen, the most unbending opponents of abortion, claim that the state should not have any abortion legislation at all, instead of declaring some abortions acceptable and some unacceptable. These men claim that Roman Catholics don't make their decisions about abortion on the basis of civil law, anyway.

CON

Religious convictions, as such, should not and constitutionally cannot be impressed on the population. However, every citizen has the responsibility—and the right—to influence legislation for the good of society. Any act which imperils the good of society requires legislation. Consider the person whose social conscience comes from religious convictions. If he is not allowed to promote his views, he becomes disenfranchised. Such an approach leaves all legislative influence in the hands of the irreligious. It is up to the populace to promote its insights, and the religious person has as much right to reflect his views in the law as the irreligious.

How do you react to the statement that abortion is murder?
PRO

I can see no essential difference between abortion and birth control, if abortion takes place before the mother can feel movement by the fetus. The fetus is not a human being; it is only *potentially* one. It is a mass of undifferentiated cells. It has no consciousness, no life experience, no knowledge. Murder is not even a remote consideration until the fetus has a chance to live outside of the mother's body. Up until the twentieth week or so, the fetus is considered to be a surgical specimen and is disposed of as such. There is no funeral, no burial.

CON

Whatever may be said about the consciousness of the fetus, the fact remains that if the human hand does not intervene, a human being will come into the world. That human would have a soul that, hopefully, would come under the destiny of God's will. I see a distinctive difference between abortion and birth control. If birth control is successful, there is no beginning of life. No potential human. No potential destiny. Abortion, on the other hand, terminates a life which has, without question, begun.

Do you believe abortion laws can be enforced?
PRO

No, because the question, from a legal point of view, is not moral. For example, a doctor may decide that continued pregnancy will so affect a woman emotionally as to cause considerable unhappiness. Such decisions are legal in some states. Where do you draw the line? How unhappy must a woman be before abortion is legal? How could a jury possibly determine the doctor's guilt?

CON

The laws which were on the statute books of most states prior to the Supreme Court ruling were difficult to enforce. However, repealing of those laws was no more a solution than repealing of laws against murder. Abortion is only one of many areas in which legal confusion exists. The solution is *better* laws, not doing away with laws.

How do you feel about abortion in cases of rape, incest, or deformation of the fetus?

PRO

I cannot understand how anyone could oppose abortion in such cases. In fact, it was the case of Mrs. Sherri Finkbine of Phoenix in 1962 that focused attention on the need for abortion law reform. You recall that she had taken thalidomide. She had to go to Sweden to obtain an abortion, and the fetus was deformed. Then, the German measles epidemic of 1963–64 resulted in the birth of some 30,000 infants with congenital defects. Other cases have aroused public sympathy, such as rape. At least 31,000 women are forcibly raped in this country each year—about 3 to 4 percent of whom become pregnant. Even the old (revised since) Model Penal Code advocated by the American Law Institute permitted abortion in three situations:

1. When it is needed to prevent grave impairment of the physical or mental health of the mother;

2. When there is substantial risk the child will be born with a grave physical or mental defect;

3. When the pregnancy results from rape or incest and there is authoritative certification.

CON

I will have to react to different parts of your question. In cases of rape or incest, adequate laws can be written. If the victim reports the crime within three or four days, the uterus is scraped for evidence of the crime, thus eliminating the possibility of pregnancy in virtually every case. If laws do not make such provision, I believe they should do so. In cases of suspicion that the fetus may be deformed, I feel differently. Already, vaccines are available to offset the danger of German measles. I believe the danger of congenital defects will lessen as research continues. But even now, I have the same basic conviction about taking a human life—though deformed—as about taking a life that is not deformed.

What about the psychological effect of abortion on a woman?

PRO

There is no evidence that abortion involves psychological hazards. Psychiatrists agree (American Psychiatric Association) overwhelmingly that such problems are negligible. A woman does not normally develop any specific feeling or attachment toward the fetus until after she feels movement. In other studies, women who had terminated pregnancies suffered no more psychiatric and neurotic symptoms than the general population. In most unmarried women, in fact, the relief is quite pronounced when an unwanted pregnancy is terminated. The same is true of young married women, and the benefits to the latter group may be important and pronounced. Legalized abortion would, in addition, take the powder out of shotgun marriages. Though I am against premarital intercourse, I am more against teen-age divorce.

CON

I believe that the studies referred to are influenced by the views of the psychiatrists and researchers who conduct them. For example, I read one psychiatrist's opinion which supported what my friend argues, only to find her asserting that those few women who demonstrated guilt feelings about abortion were victims of "fearful distortions of more complex dynamics." Such reasoning ignores contrary evidence, it seems to me.

But even if guilt feelings could be relieved with counseling, the vast majority who would never receive counseling must be considered. To require counseling before and after abortion would create a considerable bottleneck. To avoid it would leave each woman to work through her problems as best she could.

What about the rights of the unborn child?

PRO

What about the rights of the unborn child to a full life? Especially with the population explosion, no child should be brought into this world unless it has a chance at a full life. The financial and emotional resources of the parents must be utilized to best advantage. Low income people should be allowed to limit their families to the size they desire. The unborn child's rights to a full life will be *protected* by abortion, not diminished. And what about the right of the child to be *wanted?* Unwanted children account for many—perhaps most—of the problems of delinquency, maladjustment, vandalism, and violence. They grow up to be emotional cripples and criminals or misfits. Often, babies and young children are admitted to hospitals because of unmerciful beatings and torture by parents who are antagonistic toward them. Others are neglected or left for the care of children's homes. In the case of unwed mothers, even those who might be adopted must be healthy and usually must be white. There are 300,000 illegitimate children born into this country each year. Legalized abortion probably would eliminate half of that number. And families would be able to limit their families to the number they wanted and could care for.

CON

Women have highs and lows during their pregnancies. Many abortions would be performed to terminate lives of children who would, when born, be sincerely loved and wanted by their parents. Many families are very unhappy about an unexpected pregnancy; then happy beyond description with the new baby. In regard to unplanned-for children born into poor homes, history books are full of names of persons from poor homes who made significant contributions. I, too, am concerned about the problems of unwanted children; but I do not believe abortion is the answer. Let's seek solutions for our problems which will not bring on worse problems. In fact, many of the arguments for abortion do not consider that there are other solutions for most of the problems they emphasize.

And the unborn child does, indeed, have rights which must be protected. Unborn children are participants in lawsuits, and they are beneficiaries in insurance claims. But beyond these facts, the question really revolves around whether they are persons. If they are, their rights should be protected. If they are only a mass of cells, then perhaps they are not to be protected. I believe they are persons.

What about the rights of the mother?

PRO

Twenty-two percent of all *legitimate* births in the U.S. are unwanted by either the husband or the wife. Forty-two percent of the births that occur in poor homes are unwanted. I believe that abortion laws of any kind violate a woman's liberty to make her own choice as to what to do with her own body. The state should be silent on the matter of abortion. Pregnancy can be torture sometimes. It can destroy a woman's plan for her life. She should be free to determine for herself whether to bear children. We stress family planning now—and few people other than Catholics oppose birth control—but we refuse to allow abortion even in the early weeks of a pregnancy when birth control fails. Abortion is now and has always been the most widespread method of birth control in the world. About 30 million pregnancies in the world each year are terminated by abortion. Even the most effective contraceptives have a failure rate of 1.5 to 3 percent. If every married woman in the nation used the best contraceptives, there still would be from 350,000 to 700,000 unwanted children born each year. No one—including doctors, psychologists, and counselors of every kind—is more qualified to decide whether to have an abortion than the mother and father. Why should a married couple be forced to continue a pregnancy they tried to avoid in the first place? Most of the abortions in this country are performed on married women pregnant by their own husbands.

CON

The mother, of course, has rights. But she does not have the right to act as though the fetus she carries matters only as it affects her own particular life. Later, I want to talk about the implicit promise to life involved in the sex act. Just now, several other factors are appropriate to discuss.

First, abortion practiced simply as a method of birth control relieves the male of most of the responsibility so far as control of pregnancy goes. He no longer has to worry much about the results of his action. This problem is particularly important in regard to unmarried persons.

Second, abortion on demand reduces the necessity to use effective contraceptives. This reason accounts for the fact that there are so many abortions in the world. In countries like Japan, some women have two abortions a year. Birth control is practiced less because it is less essential. Continued research should be given to birth control methods. Such research will suffer if abortion becomes easy to obtain, and certainly birth control will be harder to sell.

Third, there was a time when married women were the most frequent seekers of abortions, but the ratio now has changed to about fifty-fifty between married and unmarried. Married women are using birth control measures more; while more unmarried girls are becoming pregnant.

What about the matter of poverty? How much would legalized abortion help the poor?

PRO

Abortion was available even when it was illegal to those who could pay the price and were not afraid to skirt the law. A study made in New York before passage of the state's new abortion law revealed that nine out of ten in-hospital abortions were performed on middle-class white women. Some doctors perform illegal abortions on their clients for high prices. Since these doctors charge from $350 to $1,000 for abortions, only the affluent can pay. The rest must go to the back alley if they are to have abortions. A study of deaths occurring in pregnancy and childbirth in New York a few years ago disclosed that abortion complications resulted in the deaths of almost half of the Negro women tested, 56 percent of the Puerto Rican women, and only 25 percent of the white women. These figures could relate to either poverty level, race, or both. In Hungary, deaths from abortion have declined over 80 percent since legalized abortion. Since California passed its new law, the number of legal abortions in hospitals has at least tripled.

When you consider the horror which attends illegal abortions, you cannot help but be in favor of moving the practice into hospitals. Under proper conditions, there is very little to an abortion in the early weeks of pregnancy. A dilatation and curettage (frequently called D and C) is a process which simply widens the cervix and then scrapes the lining of the uterus with a blade called a curette. It takes only about twenty minutes and a day's stay in the hospital. When the operation is performed illegally, it is usually done by amateurs who use methods which can easily produce hemorrhage. It is estimated that some one million women attempt to abort themselves with coat hangers, screw drivers, soap suds, poisons, and by other dangerous methods. About 8,000 of these women die every year as a consequence. Ironically, the sympathetic doctor who performs an abortion was subject to the same penalty, if he was caught, as the jackleg incompetent who may kill the mother.

CON

Abortion laws actually would not help the poor as much as claimed. Doctors' fees alone would eliminate the service from the poor. The coldness and humiliation which the poor frequently suffer at the hands of public hospitals (caused in part by heavy workloads) would eliminate many more. The heavy patient loads of the hospitals—already crucial—would become even more critical. I can't imagine anyone believing that the poor will receive equal treatment as the middle class and affluent under such conditions. England passed a revised abortion law in 1968 and the number of abortions skyrocketed. That nation's gynecologists are spending virtually all of their time counseling patients about abortion and performing abortions. They were trained for a more noble practice. The patients who need their training must wait in line.

Many doctors are turning against abortion because of such problems. An Oregon doctor protested, "You can't tell a cancer patient that she cannot be admitted for surgery because the beds are taken up with abortion patients." The Orange County, California, hospital declared a moratorium on abortions because of a similar problem.

Then, there is a problem with many doctors themselves who do not believe in abortion on demand. Their reluctance will, in effect, leave the market open for doctors who specialize in performing abortions, much like many doctors followed the weight-losing craze. Inevitably, their judgment would be affected when counseling with a patient about an abortion.

Looking at the experience of those countries which have legalized abortion, the problem has not helped the poor. In Sweden, for example, the number of *illegal* abortions has risen, along with the number of legal ones.

I am concerned about another problem, too, in regard to the poor. Social workers are under constant pressure to keep down welfare costs. Poor people may very well be encouraged by well-meaning case workers to obtain abortions even though the family may want the child.

Sometimes abortion is compared to mercy killing. How do you feel the two relate?

PRO

The analogy is often made in this argument between the person in a coma and the embryo or fetus. But the comparison breaks down. The person in a coma is a person, without question. He has conscious family ties. He is loved and has loved in return. He has left a mark in the world which cannot be erased. The fetus has no tangible connection with the world and, if aborted, leaves no more influence behind than does a temporary illness.

CON

I do not believe the analogy my friend referred to is really appropriate to the question. My concern is with the attitude people will develop toward life itself. If abortion becomes legalized, the public cannot but be influenced to disregard life a bit more. Some callousness is bound to result. England legalized mercy killing just two years after legalizing abortion. In fact, you can build a better case for allowing a fetus to live, with life ahead, than for a comatosed person without hope of recover, with life behind him.

You are raising the question of the effect abortion will have on society. What do you feel the influence will be?

PRO

There is no appreciable difference in attitude toward life in Japan, Sweden, and other countries that allow abortion than in this country. Family ties are strong; births, deaths, and marriages are as sacred.

Going further, abortion will actually create better conditions for our culture by eliminating much misery. Children will be born who are wanted and loved and for whom families have had the chance to make adequate provision. In such a society, life will be held in much greater sanctity.

CON

To me, this question is one of the most crucial ones. Abortion, I believe, will bring about a deterioration in public morality. After legalizing abortion, the next logical conclusion is that promiscuous sex is not wrong. Out of my own conviction as to the place of sex in life, I agree with the view that when a man and woman engage in the sex act, they are bound to the results of that act. Even though they use birth control measures to avoid pregnancy, they are obligated morally to accept pregnancy if birth control fails. Ideally, of course, they would agree consciously to accept the results. But at any rate, society needs to require the keeping of this *promise to life,* which is implicit in the sex act whether it is consciously made or not. By such a requirement, society maintains a high sexual ideal. In such an intimate relationship as sex, two partners *should* be prepared to follow through with the results of their actions, as part of their commitment to each other. Without such commitment, the home—and thus the nation—cannot survive.

What closing comments do you have?

PRO

Only that I believe abortion laws do not take into consideration the facts as they are. While I agree with my friend's idealistic view of sex and marriage, our nation is simply not on that plane. Nor will abortion bring about, in my opinion, the decline of the home. Our laws should help us solve the problems we have, and we have problems that can only be solved by legalizing abortion.

CON

I believe that laws need to be designed—in spite of the Supreme Court's opinion—to allow for abortion in case of rape or incest, and in cases of severe damage to a woman's physical or emotional health. But I believe that the laws need to be spelled out and defined in such a way that they cannot be interpreted loosely. I believe that aborting a fetus—a human life—for any other than the drastic reasons I described is morally wrong and will result in the deterioration of our society.

5

The Bible and Women's Liberation
Shirley Stephens

"Oh, I didn't think women's liberation was biblical," a friend suggested sometime ago.

I disagree with her remark. Not only do I believe there is a *biblical view* of women's liberation, I believe the Bible was the *first promoter* of women's liberation.

Obviously, the whole thing began when God created man and woman. He created them as equals, you know. Both were made in his image (Gen. 1:27). Married, they were "one flesh" (Gen. 2:24). They were partners, and as partners were given the task of ruling the earth together (Gen. 1:28). Equality for the sexes was God's original intent.

Then something happened: woman sinned; man sinned. A curse was pronounced on both of them. Part of woman's punishment was for man to rule over her. That development came about as a result of sin, not because of God's original intent. Before the fall, woman was a helpmate, not a slave or a servant. Only when sin entered the human race was she assigned an inferior role.

From the time of the fall until Christ came, a wife was considered to be the possession of her husband. She was not a *person;* she was a *thing.* The Old Testament records instances in which women exercised authority over men, but those examples are few. Society as a whole assumed that women were inferior to men. Even today, in some parts of the world and in many homes, a wife virtually is a servant with few or no rights. Some religions stress the inferior status of women (i.e., Islam, Mormonism).

Though historically women have held an inferior position to men in Christianity, our religion actually does not teach such a doctrine. Christ changed the status of women from the Old Testament concept. He lifted woman up and removed the curse caused by sin. Woman was restored to her original position of equality with man. Circumstances, however, did not permit her immediately to claim her new standing.

Paul set forth the equality of *all* persons in Christ: "There is neither Jew nor Greek, there is neither bond nor free, there is neither male nor female: for ye are all one in Christ Jesus" (Gal. 3:28, KJV).

Even though Paul did set forth the equality of every person, his writing has been used widely to keep woman "in her place." It is absolutely essential that Paul's remarks in regards to women be interpreted in light of Galatians 3:28.

Galatians 3:28 emphasizes the oneness of the body of Christ. Further, the church is one body of Christ with many members (1 Cor. 12:12). All members of that body stand before God as equals. There are different functions within the body, but all members are led by the same Spirit and are equal.

In addition to specific passages, the doctrine of the priesthood of the believer proclaims the equality of believers. Each person within the body of Christ is a priest who goes directly to God to seek his instruction and care. Each person not only has the right to be his own priest, he has the responsibility to perform that function. And other Christians have an obligation to accept the obvious leading of the Holy Spirit in a Christian's life.

When rules (written or unwritten) interfere with a believer's right to stand as a priest before God, the working of the Holy Spirit in the life of a believer is limited. When that happens, a believer's equality before God is denied.

Who has the right to close a certain area of service to a person because of sex? Who is to determine the destiny of any man or woman? God. Only God. He expresses himself through the members of his church according to *his* will and purposes. No man is to stand between the believer and God as he reveals his will.

Four facts, then, overwhelmingly demand that women be equal: God's original intent, Christ's removal of that curse of sin, the doctrine of the priesthood of the believer, and the oneness of Christ.

But there are passages in the New Testament that seem to limit the freedom of expression among women. Some of these passages relate to marriage. Marriage is a frequent subject in women's liberation advocates. Indeed, marriage cannot be excluded from woman's quest for liberation.

Ephesians 5:22–33 is the basic passage for determining marriage relationships. This passage is *not* a statement on the inferior status of women, as some have supposed. Paul did not intend such an emphasis. Rather, he set forth requirements for Christian marriage. It is true that he told the wives to submit themselves to the authority of their husbands. But he also told husbands to love their wives.

Several aspects of the wife's submission to her *own* husband need to be emphasized. First, the submission is to be to the authority of *her own husband only,* not to any other man (Col. 3:18, 1 Pet. 3:1). If a woman has training and skill that surpasses certain men, she does not have to take second place. This text does not give guidelines in general, but only for the marriage relationship.

Second, the submission is "in the Lord." A wife is not asked to go against her conscience. First Corinthians 11:3 suggests a chain of authority: God-Christ-man-woman. However, the authority of the man over the women is not the same as that of Christ over man. The claims of Christ on both man and woman limit man's authority. All relationships are under the lordship of Christ.

Third, the submission really is a matter of function. Every institution needs a head. Otherwise, nothing could be accomplished; there would be utter chaos. Just as the church can have only one head, the family must have only one head. Man is the logical choice because of his position as protector and provider. But his headship is not to be a dictatorship. His place of leadership is limited by the demands of Christ on *all members* of the family.

Fourth, a man and a woman are not independent of each other (1 Cor. 11:11–12). Woman in a sense owes her existence to man; by the same token, man owes his existence to woman. Neither has the right to claim superiority. Each must depend on the other.

Fifth, the submission is voluntary—self-subjugation, not subjugation. And it is not an "anything you do is all right" kind of self-subjugation. That is empty-headedness. A marriage which benefits only one person is not a Christian marriage.

Sixth, the submission assumes certain attitudes and actions on the part of the husband. "Husbands, love your wives," Paul said (Eph. 5:25; Col. 3:19). The word used for love in both of these passages is *agape*—the highest form of love. It is Godlike love. It is love that seeks the best for the object of one's love. A husband cannot expect a wife to submit to his leadership if he does not love her and want what is best for her. He must prove himself worthy of her trust.

A high-school teacher bragged to a group of students about how his wife had worked when he did graduate work. One of the students asked him if he helped her with the housework. "No," he replied, "that's women's work." His consideration for his wife fell far short of the *agape* love demanded of husbands.

Agape love implies that a man will love his wife as he loves himself (Eph. 5:28–29). Every man tries to satisfy his physical needs; he wants to be accepted as an individual; he wants to find fulfillment; he wants to have a sense of worth and accomplishment; he desires opportunity to progress in life; he wants to be happy. He should want no less for his wife. The question each man must ask himself is this: "What do I want for myself?" That which he wants for himself he should want for his wife as well.

Not only should the husband love his wife as he loves himself, he should love his wife as "Christ loved the church, and gave himself for it" (Eph. 5:25). A husband's love is to be sacrificial. Christ gave himself for the church. That self-giving love, not tradition or society, is the standard for the Christian husband. What woman would not be willing to submit herself to the authority of a man who loved in such a manner?

If a husband really loves his wife as Paul commanded, he will want her to develop her talents and fulfil God's will for her life. He will not demand that she conform to an image that he holds of all women. He will accept her as an individual and help her to become the person God would have her be.

Certainly, certain functions exist within the family unit that can be performed better by one or the other of the partners. Still, roles sometimes need to be adjusted. Any decisions made in regard to role sharing or changing should be made on the basis of the equality of both persons.

Marriage does place limitation on a woman, limitations that are not placed on a single woman. The married woman is not free to do anything and everything she wants to do. She must consider the needs and desires of her husband and children. Man, of course, is limited by his similar responsibilities.

One fact must not be overlooked. When Paul compared the relationship of a man and woman in marriage to the union of Christ and his church, he lifted marriage to a wonderfully high plain. And, he sought rights for women that the society of that day would not give them. Both Jews and Greeks were convinced that women were inferior in that they should occupy an inferior place in society. Under Jewish law a woman was the possession of her husband; she had no status in society. Her husband could divorce her for any reason, but she could not begin divorce proceedings against him. Paul's instructions to husbands in Ephesians 5:24 and Colossians 3:19 placed new obligations on Christian men which society did not demand.

Other passages that direct women to be in subjection to their husbands possibly indicate that the move developed among Christian women to claim their equality. Possibly, the words of Paul and Peter were written because the demands of women were creating an unfavorable witness to people outside the church. In Titus 2:5, women are instructed to be obedient to their husbands so that "No one will speak evil of the message from God" (TEV). If women had suddenly demanded equality, the society would have been convinced that Christianity corrupted women. Instead of seeing Christianity as a religion that raised morals, it would have been considered one that produced "loose women."

Peter appealed for women to be subject to their unbelieving husbands, so that wives' conduct might win husbands to Christ. An unsaved husband would have been shocked if his wife suddenly asserted herself. That assertion, in all probability, would have driven him farther away from the gospel.

All the women were equal in Christ, they could not expect to change society quickly.

In addition to the conduct of women in the marriage relationship, Paul gave some instructions for the role of women in church.

In 1 Corinthians 11:5, we find women praying and speaking in the worship service of the church. Paul's only instruction was for them to wear veils when they participated in a service. But later, in 1 Corinthians 14:34–35 and 1 Timothy 2:11, Paul told women to keep quiet in church. He also forbade them to teach or exercise authority over men. Intervening incidents must have necessitated the setting up of regulations. Possibly, as women tried to assume their position of equality in the church, those actions had caused trouble within and outside the church.

Several factors may have caused Paul's change in position:

First, Paul was a Jew. The only valid religion he knew before Christianity was the Jewish religion. In the Jewish synagogue, women did not participate actively in the worship service. Only men could pray out loud. It was logical for him to revert to that order of worship, especially if the participation of women caused trouble.

Second, the society of that day frowned on the participation of women in the leadership of the churches. "Proper" women did not speak in public in either Roman or Jewish society. Possibly, women's participation in the worship service was bringing shame to the Christian movement.

Third, Paul may have realized that few women were qualified to teach or to lead in church. Women received little or no schooling. What they did learn primarily was designed to equip them to perform wifely and family duties. There were some exceptions to this rule, but they were few.

We do know that Paul used women in places of leadership. Lydia had a church in her home. Priscilla and her husband, Aquila, were companions and fellow workers with Paul. In some references to this couple, Priscilla is mentioned first (Rom. 16:3; Acts 18:18; 2 Tim. 4:19). Priscilla did some teaching, for she and Aquila took Apollos aside and explained the word of God to him (Acts 18:26). Phoebe was a leader in the church at Cenchrea (Rom. 16:1). Thus, when women were qualified, Paul used them in places of leadership.

Traditionally in Southern Baptist churches, women are not ordained as deaconesses or ministers, although there have been one or two breakthroughs lately. Yet, this traditional stand cannot be supported by the Bible or the practice of the early church. There were deaconesses in the early church. Phoebe (Rom. 16:1) was a deaconess in the church at Cenchrea (as translated by RSV, Phillips, Lenski, Alford). She is the first deaconess mentioned in the New Testament. Then, as now, some ministries could be carried out better by women than by men.

The qualifications for deacons (1 Tim. 3:8–10) could have included women deacons. The women in 1 Timothy 3:11 easily could be women deacons, rather than wives of deacons as often is assumed. The word translated as "their wives" actually means *"women."*

Four possible interpretations have been suggested for *women:*

(1) wives of deacons, (2) deaconesses, (3) wives of bishops and deacons, (4) women in general. I believe the evidence supports the second interpretation. First, there is no feminine for *diakonos* (deacon) in the New Testament. In Romans 16:1 Phoebe is called a *diakonos* (masculine form for deacon). Second, the virtues required of women are set in a passage whose context presents specific requirements for deacons. (Here the virtues apply to leaders in the church, not wives. There are other places in the New Testament where wives are given advice about their conduct.) Third, Paul used the word meaning "women," not "their wives." If he had meant wives, he would have used the word that specifically meant wives. Incidentally, the great Southern Baptist Greek scholar, A. T. Robertson *(Word Pictures in the New Testament),* presents this view. This simple and literal translation makes the qualifications just set forth in verses 8–10 to apply to all deacons—men and women.

Of course, there is the joke question based on verse 12: "How can a woman be the husband of one wife?" This observation has been used to prove that women cannot be deacons. However, the requirements for women deacons were given along with men in 1 Timothy 3:8–11. To apply this verse to eliminate women as deaconesses ignores the plain teaching of the passage.

Paul gave directions to women in general, too, particularly in regard to dress. Just as the society of Paul's day must be considered in any discussion and decision about the role of women in church, so must be his instructions to women about their dress.

In 1 Corinthians 11:5, Paul instructed women to wear veils when they prayed or spoke God's message. In 1 Timothy 2:9 he tells women not to adorn themselves with gold, pearls, or other costly ornaments. He even instructed them not to braid their hair. Peter (1 Pet. 3:4) also stressed the importance of avoiding costly apparel and other showy adornment.

First century prostitutes did not wear veils. Only the immodest woman appeared in public without a veil. When a Christian woman did not wear a veil, she looked like the adulteress who was required to shave her head because of her sin (1 Cor. 11:5). Prostitutes also gave considerable attention to their hair. Braided hair, gold, and costly attire were the apparel of pagan women. If the Christian woman copied the pagan, she lowered rather than raised her station in life.

These instructions to women were given so that they might present a positive witness to the world. The directions also were given to stress good taste in dress in cultivation of Christian qualities. The attire mentioned in 1 Timothy 2 and 1 Peter 3 was worn to attract attention. Women were to concentrate on cultivating Christian qualities rather than outward adornment.

Few would argue that the *specifics* of dress mentioned in 1 Corinthians 11, 1 Timothy 2, and 1 Peter 3 apply today, but the abiding principles of good taste and good witness do apply today as they did in the first century.

The Bible does give guidelines on the role of women in the home, in church, and in the world. Honesty and accurate biblical interpretation demand that the passages on this subject be interpreted in light of the society in which the writers lived and in proper context. To pick a few phrases out of their biblical context and say that they represent the teaching of the Bible on any subject is unfair and is poor Bible study technique.

Yes, women's liberation *is* biblical. The New Testament testifies to that position. Paul was all for the equality of women.

So why didn't he start a movement to free women? For the same reason he did not start a movement to free the slaves. He simply did not have the time to implement every truth of the gospel. His primary task was to spread the gospel and to establish churches. Any deviation from that task would have brought harm to the cause of Christ. Just as he could not let the gospel become a "free the slaves" movement, he could not let it become a "free the women" movement. Such movements would have overshadowed the main purpose of the gospel.

Paul did not speak against slavery, but who would say that he was for slavery. Just as he told Onesimus to accept his status in life, he told women to live within the limitations of the society of that day. In time, the teachings of the Bible on personhood would be taken seriously.

Society has changed considerably from what it was in the first century. The time has come for Galatians 3:28 to be the basis for relationships in Christ. A woman stands as an equal with man. For that reason, no woman need apologize for selecting a particular vocation or position in church or soceity—if she seeks God's will in the matter.

However, as with every privilege, there are responsibilities in claiming equality. A woman is not free to assert her freedom irrespective of the feelings of other people. The new freedom actually imposes more responsibilities on a Christian woman, because so much is open to her. She must be honest in her demands. She has no right to select a certain occupation or engage in a particular activity just to prove she can claim that right.

Any exercise of women's liberation must be performed within the framework of the gospel. Christian standards of conduct must be observed. Some women liberationists see freedom as the right to engage in promiscuous sexual relationships. Others look on marriage as something evil, meant to enslave women. Still others see it as claiming a superior status to men. No biblical view of women's liberation can include such conduct or attitudes. The projection of a positive Christian witness is just as important today as it was in Paul's day. The demands of Christ must come first. As a woman gains her freedom, she cannot become a slave to sin. She therein defeats her purpose.

As I began this chapter, someone suggested: "There is no way a woman can come out on top according to the Bible." I'll have to agree with that. But I do think a woman can come out an *equal.* That is the most any sensible woman demands or expects to achieve.

6

The Future: The Mystery of Birth
Robert Dean

The year is 2001. Thirty-eight years ago, a woman gave birth to a baby. That was the last natural childbirth to occur in the civilized world.

Fantastic?

Some scientists say no. Someday, they claim, human life will be conceived in a test tube and the embryo will develop in a laboratory.

These scientists—and some of them shudder a bit when they say it—believe Aldous Huxley was not far off base in his *Brave New World*. The book (which is, by the way, decidedly non-Christian) was written forty years ago. It was fascinating and frightening, but was accepted as science fiction. In the brave new world, Huxley predicted, the word *mother* will be a grotesque reminder of an earlier period when human birth took place amid pain and blood. Only in primitive areas would the human process of birth remain.

We stand at the edge of a revolution in biology that portends changes more dramatic than those brought about by nuclear physics or space exploration. Some of the directions that research in biology may take will bring about serious moral problems. Man must walk gingerly as he steps into the future. After all, biology is the science of life. This chapter will present developments in biology and raise some cautions of concern to Christians.

Biologists long have been looked upon as absent-minded professors who dissect frogs and study bird migrations. This Gordon Rattray Taylor points out in *The Biological Time Bomb*. He shatters this stereotype as he describes the fantastic new revolution about to take place. Like a time bomb, he claims, the revolution is soon to explode, blasting its fragments in many directions.

The fact that Huxley ignored God in his *Brave New World* is reason enough to discount him as a prophet. Nevertheless, he is not the first writer to come close to glimpsing the future. Jules Verne did so in his novels. And comic strip characters Flash Gordon and Buck Rogers have been replaced by real space travelers. Few people talk about the impossible anymore. The biological revolution, though, tampers with the future in a more crucial way than any of these other changes: It tampers with the control of human life. Control is possible by changing the methods of human reproduction; by controlling or manipulating genes, thus controlling heredity; and by manufacturing men in strange new ways. The possibilities raise three important questions:

1. Will human life be conceived in test tubes and developed under laboratory conditions?

2. Will man control his destiny by controlling his heredity?

3. Will new ways of making men be used to make new kinds of men?

These three questions in turn raise three other questions of special concern to Christians:

1. What is the future of marriage and parenthood?

2. At what point does man move beyond his divine commission to have dominion, and start attempting to play God?

3. What are the unique qualities of human life with which man should not tamper?

The biological revolution already has begun in regard to human reproduction: The Pill has been developed; fertility has been restored to some infertile men and women; and artificial insemination has accounted for thousands of human births. Each of these developments has opened up new horizons in sex and reproduction. But they also have posed new moral—and in some cases, legal—questions. Those who predict an increased biological revolution insist that bigger changes are on the way.

Today's contraceptive pill is only a forerunner of more sophisticated methods of birth control. The regulation of fertility will become easier and more precise with pills, injections, or implantations whose effect will last for weeks, months, and even years. Scientists even are changing the vocabulary. Instead of *birth* control, they will refer to *fertility* control. With the new methods, fertility either can be stopped or stimulated.

Artificial insemination (AI) has been with us for over a decade. Exact statistics are unavailable, but it is estimated that at least 150,000 Americans have been conceived in this manner. The procedure is used to cause pregnancy when the union of sperm with egg either is unlikely or impossible. In artificial insemination, sperm generally is obtained from the husband (AIH). But in some cases, the sperm is obtained from an anonymous donor (AID). AID has been made possible by the ability of scientists to preserve sperm over a long period of time. AID ordinarily is used only when attempts at inducing pregnancy using the husband's sperm have failed.

Society has not yet solved the moral and legal questions raised by artificial insemination, particularly when an anonymous donor is involved.

And artificial insemination is only a start. Scientists are predicting a new process: artificial inovulation. This procedure involves implanting a fertilized egg in the uterus of a woman. The egg may be obtained from the woman's own body, or it may come from a donor.

Scientists already have been able, under laboratory conditions, to fertilize eggs with sperm. Also, they have been able to flush fertilized eggs from a woman's body without damaging the eggs. Both of these procedures may be used in artificial inovulation. Scientists predict that it will be only a matter of time until they discover how to implant a fertilized egg in a woman's uterus, where it would grow as in a normal pregnancy.

David M. Rorvik has tried to make artificial inovulation appealing to the women who read *McCall's* magazine. He called his article "Artificial Inovulation: A Startling New Way to Have a Baby." Artificial inovulation, Rorvik explains, can enable childless couples to have children. A young wife with a health problem may not be strong enough to bear children. A doctor may remove a fertilized egg from her uterus and implant it in the womb of another woman who would bear the child for her. Another woman may be able to bear children, but is sterile. A doctor may implant a fertilized egg, given by an anonymous donor, in her womb. The embryo would grow in the uterus of the woman who was sterile. She would thereby be the mother in every way except that the egg and sperm would be from unknown donors. The process thus becomes an adoption, but one that takes place just after fertilization rather than just after birth: *prenatal adoption.*

Rorvik does not fail to point out some problems that may arise from prenatal adoption. In the first situation, artificial inovulation, for example, what would happen if the woman who bore the child became so attached to the child that she refused to give it up?

The term "test-tube babies" has been applied to artificial insemination. Doubtless, the same term will be used about artificial inovulation when that process becomes possible, especially when egg and sperm are fertilized under laboratory conditions. However, "test-tube baby" better describes yet another phase of the biological revolution: the entire development of a human fetus *outside* the body of the mother. Some scientists predict that a kind of artificial placenta will make such a practice possible.

Dr. Daniele Petrucci, an Italian scientist and surgeon, began such an experiment in 1959. He fertilized an egg and began to grow an embryo. The first press reports of his work caused such a furor that Petrucci terminated the experiment at the end of twenty-nine days. He has reported that the embryo in a similar experiment survived for fifty-nine days. Scientists admit that many technical problems remain to be solved before a fetus can fully develop outside a woman's body. But they predict that it will be done.

Many people have strong reservations about the kind of experiments necessary to develop this phase of the biological revolution. Some scientists have tried to offset these objections by pointing out the practical uses of an effective artificial placenta. For example, an artificial placenta would serve something of the same purpose that incubators now serve in saving the lives of the prematurely born. If a therapeutic abortion were necessary to save the life of a mother, the fetus could be transferred to a machine in which it would continue to grow and develop.

If the test-tube baby concept develops, a new branch of medicine relating to the care of the fetus will develop along with it. Already, medical scientists can observe and treat fetuses in a limited way while they are in the womb. But a fetus developing in a machine could be more easily observed. New methods of surgery and treatment could develop. In addition, the fetus could be protected from defects caused by harmful drugs and viruses in the mother's system.

Prophets of the new biology predict that the process, if developed, may revolutionize childbearing. Apart from the medical values, women will be freed from the discomforts and limitations of pregnancy. Thus, some women might choose this new method of childbearing purely for the sake of convenience. Some biologists even predict that the *normal* method of childbearing might become the exception rather than the rule.

We cannot help asking: "What will be the final result of this phase of the biological revolution? Will our world someday become like Huxley's *Brave New World?*" According to Huxley, the family will disappear. The state will control all of life. Babies will be produced in laboratories and then carefully conditioned in state nurseries. Contraceptives will be so foolproof that pregnancy will be almost unheard of, although sexual prosmicuity will be the normal pattern of life.

Is the family on the way out? No one can deny that the family already is in trouble. the current sexual revolution has shaken the very foundation of marriage. And many homes are failing also in the vital task of rearing children. Some scientists predict that the biological revolution may drive the final nails in the coffin of the traditional view of the family.

Such frightening prospects alarm the Christian. He wonders: "Is the process inevitable? Can nothing be done?"

Albert Rosenfeld, the science editor of *Life* magazine, is one who expects to see drastic changes in sex and marriage. In his book, *The Second Genesis: the Coming Control of Life,* Rosenfeld seems to expect the end of marriage and parenthood as we know it. However, he does not completely rule out their survival: "Love, marriage, and the family have been around a long time, and have served us well. But it is clear that they may not survive the new era unless we really want them to." [1]

Unless we really want them to! These are the key words.

Life magazine hired Louis Harris and Associates to poll a sample of representative adults on the new methods of reproduction. One thing revealed by the poll (reported in the June 13,1969 issue of *Life*) is that few people are aware of the coming revolution. Only 3 percent even knew about artificial insemination before the poll. In spite of this unfamiliarity, many people showed a remarkable willingness to accept the new methods whenever they promised to contribute to family betterment. For example, only 19 percent approved the general idea of artificial insemination with the sperm of a donor. But 35 percent approved of this method if it was the only way in which a wife could bear a child. Or take the general idea of growing a baby outside a mother's womb. The percentage of approval went up from 25 to 33 percent when it was stipulated that the wife or child might be endangered by normal childbirth.

The most encouraging finding of the *Life* poll is that many people are still committed to preserving family life and marital faithfulness. The people questioned by Louis Harris and Associates made it plain that they were anxious to strengthen, not weaken, the bonds of love and family.

However, one aspect of the poll's findings is disturbing. Many people have no clear-cut guidelines for deciding what actually will strengthen or weaken the bonds of love and family. Therefore, they either may naively accept or blindly reject what science makes available.

It is at the point of discerning values and hindrances to marriage and family that Christians can offer help to society in coping with these revolutionary methods of human reproduction. If Christians are on their toes, many people may be led to a new understanding of, appreciation of, and commitment to the abiding principles of Christian family life.

Many Christians still are largely unaware of the biological revolution. Therefore, only a few have given serious thought to applying biblical teachings to these revolutionary methods of human reproduction.

Paul Ramsey is one of the few who has published his views on this subject. He is a professor of Christian ethics. His book, *Fabricated Man,* reflects the study and thought Ramsey has given to setting forth some guidelines for coping with the biological revolution. Ramsey deserves a hearing—if for no other reason than that he has made a careful and thoughtful study of this subject. And he has taken the Bible seriously in forming his conclusion.

Understanding Ramsey's conclusions at every point is not easy, but one of his main points appears to be that parenthood, when it occurs, should grow out of the one-flesh unity of a husband and a wife. Thus, he accepts any method that makes parenthood possible in this context. And he opposes any method that disrupts this one-flesh unity, which Ramsey interprets as the sexual union of husband and wife.

Ramsey believes, then, that the new methods are valid under certain circumstances. For example, artificial insemination may be valid when the husband's sperm is used if this is the only way for a couple to have a child. By the same token, artificial inovulation using the wife's egg and the husband's sperm may also be valid in cases of infertility. And under certain conditions, an artificial placenta for a fetus may serve a therapeutic value for the fetus or the mother.

But Ramsey opposes the use of each of these methods when the sperm and/or egg come from someone other than the married couple. He believes that this tends to disrupt the one-flesh union of man.

Not every Christian agrees with Ramsey. Some believe that he allows too much freedom in choice of reproduction methods. Others think that he has not allowed enough choice. Most Christians agree that a line must be drawn. But they do not agree where to draw the line.

Michael Hamilton believes that Ramsey's line is too narrow and restricted. Christian parenthood, Hamilton claims, does not require all children to come from the sperm and egg of the married couple. He sees the primary Christian guideline not in how the children are *conceived* but in how they *raised.*

Hamilton writes: "I believe that the demand of love in relation to parenthood is fulfilled in ensuring that all children born into this world, by whatever means, be reared in a family. Parenthood in its deepest sense is not a biological but a human function—of a man and wife accepting responsibility for caring for and rearing a child, thus, in my opinion, A.I.D. is legitimate for some parents." [2]

It is probably too early in the discussion to say who is more nearly correct—Ramsey or Hamilton. Many Christians are just beginning to become aware of this area. The whole subject is so new to most of us that we have not yet had time to digest all the facts, to restudy biblical principles, and to discuss with fellow Christians how biblical principles apply.

But some conclusions immediately are obvious when a Christian views the possible new approaches to human reproduction. Christians cannot afford to be uninformed. Neither can we be uninvolved in the direction of modern society. Otherwise, these new methods could destroy marriage and the family, and usher in the kind of state control of human reproduction described in *Brave New World*. Our best hope—and perhaps our only hope—of avoiding something very much like Huxley's world lies with people of moral and spiritual conviction who are willing to become informed about the discoveries and predictions of science. And these Christians will help scientists and society as a whole discover some adequate guidelines for coping with new developments.

This chapter has dealt with only one aspect of the biological revolution's coming control of life. These new methods of reproduction will give rise to the possibility to controlling human life by controlling heredity. The predictions in the area of heredity control are even more amazing than those in the area of reproduction: the possibility of predetermining the sex of a child; egg banks, sperm banks, and frozen embryos used as a basis for selective human breeding; and changing the structure of the genes in such a way as to control what a person will be and even to remake the human race! And so we move to the next chapter.

---

[1] Albert Rosenfeld, *The Second Genesis: The Coming Control of Life* (Englewood Cliffs, N.J.: Prentice-Hall, Inc., 1959), p. 182.

[2] Michael Hamilton, "New Life for Old: Genetic Decisions," *The Christian Century*, May 28, 1969, p. 743.

7

The Future: A Second Genesis?
Robert Dean

The housewife of the future may walk into a medical commissary, armed with a doctor's prescription or a license. She will look over rows of labeled packages, like those flower seeds come in. But each package will contain a frozen, specially bred one-day-old embryo. Labels will certify the embryonic child to be free from genetic defects and will tell about his probable characteristics.[1] This housewife is shopping for a baby. The embryo she selects will be medically implanted by a doctor in her uterus and she will nurture the embryo to birth.

Impossible?

Albert Rosenfeld, the science editor of *Life* magazine, so describes one biologist's speculations about the future control of heredity in his book, *The Second Genesis: The Coming Control of Life.* Rosenfeld cites the predictions of many prophets of the biological revolution. He concludes that the question of heredity control is not *if,* but *when.*

Rosenfeld believes that the biological revolution will make possible a "Second Genesis," in which a new man will emerge. The new man will be made in the physical image determined by his predecessor. The control of heredity will play a key role—perhaps *the* key role—in the "Second Genesis."

The question this chapter considers is: *Can man control his destiny by controlling his heredity?*

According to Rosenfeld, some scientists answer this question clearly and strongly, yes. But not all scientists, he admits, are convinced of the yes answer to each of the questions. Some biologists are openly skeptical about some of the far-out predictions of their fellow scientists. But scarcely anyone denies that the future offers greater possibilities of heredity control in one form or another.

Scientists proposed several methods to control heredity: (1) separation of the kinds of sperm that determine sex; (2) prenatal treatment of the embryo and fetus; (3) selective breeding of the human race; (4) and engineering human development by manipulating the building blocks of the body that determine heredity.

The new methods of human reproduction discussed in chapter 7 will be used to control heredity. After the housewife shopper selects an embryo, it may artificially be implanted in her body. Or it may be placed in an artificial womb. In either case, the child will not inherit her characteristics or her husband's. Instead, the child will retain the characteristics of the sperm and egg donors.

Frozen embryos pose great social and moral dilemmas that become even greater when the embryo is used in a program of heredity control. Artificial inovulation and artificial wombs are shocking enough. Using such methods *to control the destiny of mankind* is even more shocking!

New methods of *reproduction* raise questions about the nature of sex, marriage, and the family. New methods of *heredity control* raise even more profound questions. For example: At what point does man move beyond his God-given commission to have dominion and begin to play God?

We will return to this question later. But first, consider these various proposals for the control of heredity:

1. Dr. Landrum B. Shettles of New York's Columbia-Presbyterian Medical Center, along with David M. Rorvik, recently published a book called *Your Baby's Sex: Now You Can Choose.*[2]

Dr. Shettles is one of several scientists who have sought ways to accurately predetermine an embryo's sex, a pastime that has occupied man in nonscientific ways for centuries.

Dr. Shettles discovered that sperm comes in two sizes: the smaller, round-headed sperm carries the male-producing chromosomes; the larger, oval-shaped sperm carry the female-producing chromosomes. Dr. Shettles further found that at certain times during a woman's cycle a female-producing sperm, and at other times a male-producing sperm, has the best chance of fertilizing the egg. Based on this discovery, he is able to make several suggestions to couples who want to predetermine the sex of their children. Thus far, Dr. Shettles claims a high percentage of success in using this technique.

However, scientists are still looking for a technique that is 100 percent effective. Many predict that a way will be found to control which kind of sperm fertilizes the egg. When a way is found to separate the two kinds of sperm, artificial insemination may be used to induce pregnancy using a selected kind of sperm. Or the egg could be fertilized under laboratory conditions with the proper kind of sperm; then the fertilized egg could be implanted by artificial inovulation.

In addition to the obvious advantage for parents, diseases such as hemophilia that are limited to one sex could be bred out of the human race.

According to Dr. Shettles, predetermining the sex of children also will help to control the population explosion. Many couples want a boy and a girl. Often, when the second child is of the same sex as the first, they try a third time. If sex could be predetermined, many couples would be satisfied with only two children.

However, some people fear the long range results of this power to predetermine sex. Nature maintains a delicate balance between the number of male and female births, a balance that human control might upset. The imbalance could result in widespread social, moral, and political repercusions.

2. In the previous chapter, some predictions were mentioned concerning prenatal medicine. Scientists already can fertilize eggs with sperm under laboratory conditions. They expect some day to

be able to grow the fertilized egg as an embryo outside a mother's womb. This development will enable scientists to observe and treat the growing embryo and fetus.

In the baby factories of *Brave New World,* Aldous Huxley predicted that there will be an elaborate process designed to control the characteristics of the embryo. The Hatching and Conditioning Centers will do more than fertilize the eggs and develop the embryos. A special group of technicians called *Predestinators* will actually predetermine what kind of person the embryo will become.

If and when embryos and fetuses can be developed outside the mother's womb, prenatal care will become an important branch of medicine. And some of the more zealous advocates of heredity control will try to act like the Predestinators of Huxley's book.

The French biologist, Dr. Jean Rostand, for example, predicts that it will be possible to change not only the subject's sex but also the color of his eyes, the general proportions of the body and limbs, and perhaps even his facial features.

This kind of human manipulation raises some important moral questions. Is man overstepping his role and presuming to play God?

3. The late Dr. Hermann J. Muller, winner of the Nobel Prize in physiology and medicine, proposed *germinal choice* several years ago. Muller criticized the current anonymous donor practice in artificial insemination. His rather drastic proposal called for parents to forego their personal desires to reproduce their own characteristics in their children. Instead, Muller proposed establishing sperm banks from a select group of men chosen for their physical fitness and mental ability. The sperm banks would carry complete records on the donors. Then couples could select sperm donors on the basis of the characteristics they desire for their offspring.

If the day comes when eggs as well as sperm can be stored over long periods of time, the possibilities will be almost limitless.

Suppose this predicted development is attained. A couple will select an egg and sperm (which will become their child) from a wide assortment of donors. Information about each donor will be supplied with each egg and sperm. The donors may live in widely separated parts of the world. They may even live at different times.

A further sophistication of this technique is frozen embryo banks. After fertilization, the embryo is frozen and preserved. A careful record is kept of the characteristics of each parent.

Such a technique would be a boon to animal breeding. The embryos from pedigree animals could be transferred to the wombs of less well-bred animals. The resulting offspring would retain all the prizewinning characteristics of their genetic parents.

The possibility of applying this technique to mankind was the basis of the bizarre prediction about a mother shopping for an embryo as she might do for a package of seeds. Many scientists doubt that a housewife ever will select an embryo under these supermarket conditions. But scientists do take seriously the prediction that a couple will consult with a doctor about the kind of child they want. The doctor then will help them select an embryo.

Muller was optimistic about the value of germinal choice. He believed that it would be a way to breed out genetic defects and weaknesses. In the long run, he expected this kind of heredity control to breed good and desirable characteristics into the human race.

Many people have strong moral objections to this kind of heredity control. Even apart from the moral questions, some people are wary of trying to improve the human race by selective breeding. Germinal choice may cause more harm than good, they insist. Selective breeding runs the risk of breeding out some *desirable* characteristics in the process of trying to breed in certain other characteristics.

Human control of heredity by breeding is at the mercy of many variable and complex factors. Gordon Rattray Taylor points out that any attempt to improve the quality of the human race by germinal choice would be "a hit-and-miss business." He illustrates his case with a "doubtless apocryphal story" about George Bernard Shaw. The dancer Isadora Duncan once proposed to Shaw that they should have a baby. She argued, "Think of a child with my body and your mind." Shaw replied, "Ah, but suppose it had *my* body and *your* mind!"[3]

4. But there is another approach to heredity control that appeals to many scientists because it seems to promise to be more exact than germinal choice. This other approach is called *genetic engineering*. Genetic engineering is an attempt to tinker with the genes—the heredity carrying component in the sperm and egg. A variety of possible ways exist to manipulate the genes so that man, in essence, can become the master of his own heredity.

Dr. Edward Tatum of the Rockefeller Institute is one of the prophets of genetic engineering. He optimistically foresees the day when geneticists will be able to delete undesirable genes, insert others, and mechanically or chemically transform still others.

Some scientists point to factors that they believe will make impossible any kind of genetic engineering. But other scientists join Tatum in predicting that a program of genetic engineering will become a reality. Some point to the year 2000 as the date when this will happen. Others claim that the process may come about within a decade or two—if an aggressive program of research is sustained.

If and when genetic engineering becomes possible, scientists predict major breakthroughs in dealing with genetic defects and genetically-based diseases.

Leroy G. Augenstein, a biophysicist at Michigan State University, points out that the percentage of babies born with serious genetic defects is increasing. One percent of live births are so defective that they never know they are human beings. Another one percent are so defective that they never can hold a job or get married. Another four to six percent are defective enough not to be considered normal. In other words, one out of every twelve to seventeen babies is genetically defective. Augenstein estimates that within a few generations one out of ten children will be seriously defective in one way or another.

According to Joshua Lederberg, biologist at Stanford, many common diseases have a genetic origin. He estimates that from one-fourth to one-half of human disease may fall in this category. Therefore, he advocates genetic engineering to deal not only with defects associated with faulty genes, but also to deal with the many common diseases that have a genetic base.

The process of trying to control heredity in order to get rid of defects and diseases is called *negative eugenics.* Any one of the methods of heredity control might be used in a program of negative eugenics. For example, predetermining the sex of a child could be used to get rid of such diseases as hemophilia. Prenatal treatment also could be used to treat defects and diseases, germinal choice, or genetic engineering.

Positive eugenics is the attempt to improve the human race by means of heredity control. Prenatal surgery and germinal choice offer some possibilities in this area.

The most optimistic prophets of the biological revolution prefer to use genetic engineering in a program of positive eugenics. They predict that man's ability to engineer human development will enable science to make the human race more intelligent, more talented, and even more virtuous.

Generally speaking, the idea of negative eugenics has met with more public acceptance than positive eugenics. A poll conducted by Louis Harris for *Life* magazine reveals that people are willing to accept new methods that promise to decrease birth defects. But the poll showed a strong opposition to the idea of trying to produce superior people through genetics. *Life* reports: "The very suggestion raises specters of Hitler and Frankenstein in many minds." [4]

Paul Ramsey, a Methodist professor of Christian ethics, draws an important distinction between treating individual human patients and trying to treat the human race as a whole.

Under certain circumstances, Ramsey sees some kinds of genetic treatment as valid medical treatment. It may be the only available medical treatment for a serious defect. In such a case, the people involved consider the risks and make a decision. The hazards are accepted as they would be in any kind of medical treatment.

However, Ramsey warns that it is a very different thing to try to improve the human species by genetic engineering. He strongly objects to this for several reasons.

For one thing, genetic engineering may produce more harm than help for the human race. In tampering with the genes, scientists may remove some good characteristics in the process. And the process may also produce some very serious side effects. Although some scientists believe that genetic engineering will someday be less hit-and-miss than germinal choice, impatient experimenters may not be willing to wait.

The real results of genetic engineering, says Leroy Augenstein, will not be known for a generation after the actual experiments, the time needed to discover if normal offspring are born to people whose genes have been tampered with. He warns, "We would have a whole generation with extensive genetic changes *before we even knew they were in trouble.*" [5]

Not many Christian groups have faced the question of genetic engineering. The Quakers are one group that has. A committee of Quakers made this recommendation: "We believe that society must examine the implications of the new science of genetic engineering and set limits on its application lest the ability to direct human evolution produce social and moral consequences disastrous to the future of man." [6]

But even if genetic engineering becomes accurate and effective, some fundamental objections remain. The obvious practical questions are these: "Who will decide what positive qualities to instill in the human race? And who will control the process?" Or to spell it out further: "Who is it that we will appoint to play the role of God for us? Which scientist—which statesman, artist, judge, poet, theologian, philosopher, educator—and of which nation, race or creed?" [7]

Such decisions would indeed require Godlike qualities of wisdom and goodness. Paul Ramsey is among those who believe that man is neither wise enough nor good enough to seek to bring about a second genesis.

Man's history bears Ramsey out.

Ramsey says: "Men ought not to play God before they learn to be men, and after they have learned to be men they will not play God." [8]

According to the book of Genesis, God gave dominion over creation to man (Gen. 1:28). The meaning and extent of this dominion has raged each time science has made a new discovery. Some people have tried to completely separate God's work from man's work. God's work, they claim, is only that which man cannot do for himself. Therefore as science enables man to do more and more, God's work becomes less and less. Thus, each new discovery of science is criticized as an attempt to play God.

A more enlightened view has interpreted most of the discoveries of science as fulfilments of the Genesis commission to have dominion. The Bible calls man to join God in what God is doing. Medical science has been following God's leadership in pushing back the boundaries of disease. They have not been playing God; they have been carrying out a God-given role for man.

Is genetic engineering a fulfilment of this God-given commission for man to have dominion? Or is it an assertion of human pride that presumes to play God by remaking man in a second genesis?

Leroy Augenstein says that to a certain extent we all play God: "Every time a surgeon picks up a scalpel to correct a defect in a person, he is playing God. Every time a minister tries to manipulate a parishioner's basic concepts, he is playing God. In fact, each of us is here right now because two people played God—they procreated a life; nothing is more sacred than that." [9] He only muddies the water with such a broad definition. His examples describe men cooperating with God. And healing, teaching, and procreating are in a different category from a program to remake the human race in a new image.

Many Christians probably will agree with the distinction made by Paul Ramsey. The new methods of heredity control offer opportunities for good or evil. Scientists play God if they try to remake man. Doctors do not play God if the same methods are used to treat defects and diseases in individuals.

One way in which science promises to be of real help is in genetic counseling. Already, doctors can predict with considerable accuracy the chances of a child having any one of a large number of defects. The process is complicated, but further research may increase the accuracy, thus alerting a couple precisely to the danger of bearing defective children. The problem of the population explosion already has helped to create a sense of responsibility about bringing a large number of children into the world. A program of genetic counseling could help to create a climate of genetic responsibility.

Suppose that a Christian young couple learns through genetic counseling that there is a strong possibility that they will reproduce diseased or defective children. What would be the responsible thing for them to do? Would they have the right to take the risk of bringing such children into the world? Ramsey insists that Christian teachings always have childbearing as a responsibility to future generations.

Under such conditions, most Christians would decide not to have children of their own. In the future, some might seek to have a child through one of the sophisticated new methods of human reproduction—for example, prenatal adoption through artificial inovulation. Other Christian couples will apply, as they now do, for adoption of a child already in the world who needs parents to care for him.

But the biological revolution raises more bizarre possibilities and moral dilemmas than these we have discussed. The next chapter will deal with some predictions about the strange kinds of men science someday will be able to create: Making exact copies of a person by a bizarre form of reproduction that does not use two sex cells. Using a sophisticated kind of genetic engineering to make strange new shapes of men designed to explore space. Making hybrids of men and animals and of men and machines.

---

[1] Albert Rosenfeld, *The Second Genesis: The Coming Control of Life* (Englewood Cliffs, New Jersey: Prentice-Hall, Inc., 1969), p. 125.

[2] New York: Dodd Mead and Co., Inc., 1970.

[3] Gordon Rattray Taylor, *The Biological Time Bomb* (New York: The New American Library, Inc., 1968), p. 177.

[4] Louis Harris, "The Life Poll," *Life* (June 13, 1969), p. 53.

[5] Leroy Augenstein, *Come, Let Us Play God* (New York: Harper and Row, Publishers, 1969), pp. 103–104.

[6] *Who Shall Live? Man's Control Over Birth and Death* (New York: Hill and Wang, Inc., 1970), p. 70.

[7] Rosenfeld, *op. cit.*, p. 144.

[8] Paul Ramsey, *Fabricated Man: The Ethics of Genetic Control* (New Haven: Yale University Press, 1970), p. 138.

[9] Augenstein, *op. cit.*, p. 12.

8

The Future: Man-Made Men?
Robert Dean

The time is 1975. The scene is the space center at Houston. A young man is being interviewed. After careful screening, he has been selected for an unusual purpose. One hundred of his body cells will be used to reproduce one hundred children who will be exact copies of the young man. When these offspring reach maturity, they will begin to colonize the moon.

You may find this hard to believe. But David M. Rorvik began an article in *Science Digest* with this exact illustration. His article was called "Cloning: Asexual Human Reproduction." [1] Rorvik was not writing science fiction. Some scientists predict that this kind of reproduction will be possible in the future. Rorvik admits that 1975 may not be a realistic forecast, but he assures us that cloning is coming.

In this chapter we will consider some of the more bizarre predictions about "man-made men." The question is: "Will new ways of making men be used to make new kinds of men?"

Rorvik's article in *Science Digest* highlights one of the kinds of man-made men—*cloned people*. A clone is a genetically uniform mass of cells. The body of an adult contains billions of cells. Yet all these cells have a common ancestry—a single fertilized egg. Thus each cell in the body—not just the cells of sexual reproduction—has a set of chromosomes precisely identical to those in the fertilized egg cell. In other words, each cell contains the same genetic information. This information controls human heredity. If a way could be found to reproduce using body cells, the children would be exact copies of the adult donor of the cell. Some scientists predict that a way will be found to make this possible.

Dr. Frederick C. Steward of Cornell University has been successful in achieving cloning, using the lowly carrot plant. Steward bypassed the sexual process of pollination in reproducing carrots. He used single cells from the body of a mature carrot. He bathed these in nutrients and grew from them carrot plants identical to the parent cell donor. Similar experiments also have been successful with tobacco plants.

Because of the greater complexity of animal and human cells, a more complex process will be needed. Dr. J. B. Gurdon of Oxford University found a process that works with frogs. He took the nuclei out of some of a frog's intestinal cells. Then he replaced the nucleus of an unfertilized frog egg with the nucleus of an intestinal cell. Egg cells treated in this way produced tadpoles identical to the body-cell donor.

Will cloning of human beings ever be possible? Dr. Joshua Lederberg of Stanford University believes that it will. He predicts that some day body cell banks will replace sperm, egg, and embryo banks. He believes that cloning will become the preferable method of controlling reproduction and heredity.

Cloning will provide a more precise method of genetic control and germinal choice. Cloning, if successful, will eliminate unknown hereditary factors. The adult cell donor will provide the only body cells involved. In other words, there will not be two sexual cells from different individuals. In cloning, all the offspring will have exactly the same genetic qualities, in the same way that identical twins do.

Take the case of the hypothetical moon colonists. The cell donor is the living model of what each of the offspring will be. Articles on cloning often have featured this possibility of "carbon copy" people. Scientists. Athletes. Entertainers. Politicians. From any one of these could be reproduced any number of cloned offspring. Imagine, if you can, a hundred Albert Einsteins. Or Mickey Mantles. Or Dean Martins. Or Richard Nixons.

Some scientists have been advocating various approaches to improving the human race. Cloning seems to them an ideal technique to use. Cloning of selected people would be used to increase the intelligence and strength of the race.

I cannot help but raise the question of control at this point. As in the case of any program for improving the human race, who will select the persons to be body-cell donors? Imagine what use Adolf Hitler could have made of this technique!

Some scientists claim that a large number of clonal twins would have certain advantages. From a medical point of view, organ and tissue transplants could be carried out much more easily. The body of the recipient would be less likely to reject the transplant. From a practical point of view, the members of a clonal group—like twins or triplets—should be able to work in close and sympathetic cooperation with one another. For example, the 100 moon colonists should be able to function as a real team.

This, of course, is only theory. No one knows how this many "twins" would feel about themselves. And how would they act toward one another and toward the rest of society?

At the very least, each twin would face some kind of crisis of selfhood and identity. Real twins often experience something of this. Imagine having ninety-nine twin brothers!

No one knows how this group would work together if an identity crisis developed. But suppose that they were able to cooperate and work closely together. Another question remains: How would one clonal group feel about members of another close-knit clonal group? Even Joshua Lederberg, one of the enthusiastic interpreters of cloning, admits that clonism might replace racism as a social problem.

Advocates of cloning point to some values to an individual. Cloning might be used to avoid some genetic defects and diseases. For example, if a man is the carrier of a serious recessive defect, he could not risk having children through sexual procreation. Otherwise, his recessive defect might be matched by his wife. Then the trait would become dominant in their children. However, the man could have a cloned offspring and avoid this danger because the only cell involved would be his own.

But would this supposed "advantage" be outweighed by other factors? Suppose that a father does have a cloned child. What problems would this present to father and son? What problems of selfhood and identity would the son experience? As he grew toward manhood, what problems would be involved in discovering and asserting himself as a personality distinct from his father?

All of these questions are part of a larger question—What is man? But before turning directly to this question, let us look at some other proposed ways of producing man-made men.

Within the last few years, many people have read about the idea of creating life in a test tube. Some scientists believe that they will be able to create life from inorganic (nonliving) matter. In fact, this kind of synthesis of life has been suggested as a national scientific goal. This proposal was made in 1965 by the newly elected president of the American Chemical Society, Charles Price.

Some preliminary steps have already been taken in this process. However, a complete living cell has not yet been created from nonliving matter. Some people—including some scientists—believe that this will never be possible.

Some Christians have denied this possibility on theological grounds. They just don't believe that anyone but God could create life—even the simplest form of life. They might be right.

However, if scientists were to create a simple form of life, would this disprove God? A. E. Wilder Smith does not believe that it would. Smith is professor of pharmacology at the University of Illinois Medical Center. As a man of faith in God, he believes that the "creation" of life in a test tube would only be thinking God's thoughts after him. Man would only have succeeded in discovering the formula God used in creating life.

If scientists can create simple forms of life, will they then also be able to create higher forms of life? Will they be able to create a man?

Charles Price does not rule out this possibility. But he does admit that the creation of a higher form of life would involve at least as big a step beyond creating a simple form of life as the creation of the simple form of life was in the first place.

Actually, scientists do not foresee this as an approach to creating man. There are too many ways to make men using living matter for scientists to tackle the formidable task of making a man from nonliving matter.

You are in for a shock when you read about the proposed kinds of man-made men. Put your mind in neutral for a minute. Try to picture a man without legs, dressed in white, manning a small flying saucer. Or picture a man with four spider-like legs reaching out from a central torso. His eyes stand out on stems.

These are two examples of the kinds of men who may be the astronauts of the twenty-first century. The first man was predicted by a British scientist, the late J. B. S. Haldane. According to Haldane, the legless man will be manufactured under pressure in an artificial womb after his genetic material has been alerted by laser beams. He will be made to take long space journeys in a small space capsule. Therefore, he will be made without legs because legs would only get in his way in his work.

The other man will be specially bred for life on Jupiter. Jupiter contains a high pressure atmosphere. The four-legged man will be made to withstand this kind of high pressure.

Sophisticated approaches to genetic engineering and prenatal treatment will make possible such controlled mutations. Add cybernetics to these other techniques, and you have the possibility of cyborgs. Cybernetics is the study of the relationship between computing machines and the human nervous system. A *cyborg* is a computerized man, a *cybernetic organism.*

The word *cyborg* sometimes is used in a general sense of any combination of man and machine. In this sense, a cyborg covers the use of prosthetic devices. A prosthetic device is controlled at will by the mind of the wearer. For example, such a device is now available for artificial arms for amputees. Such an arm is so integrated into the body's nervous system that it is controlled at will.

Some scientists predict that this principle will be used to create all kinds of combinations of men and machines. The cyborgs of the future will be very sophisticated and complex. For example, the ultimate may be a human brain in a machine that is controlled by the brain. The machine would be so built as to provide greater strength, diversity, and range than a human body.

Various kinds of human mutations would be bred to fit various prosthetic devices. The legless man, for example, could be joined to his space capsule.

If this sounds weird, consider the predictions about *hybrids*. Some scientists predict that human and animal genetic material could be mixed in making a new kind of man! Or a new kind of animal? The official term for such a being is a *chimera*. The name comes from Greek mythology. A chimera was a composite monster of some kind.

Lederberg predicts: "Before long we are bound to hear of tests of the effect of dosage of the human twenty-first chromosome on the development of the brain of the mouse or gorilla." [2] Such a technique could be used to produce man-animal chimeras of varying proportions of human, subhuman, and hybrid tissue. A panel of highly respected scientists recently predicted that these creatures will be created in order to perform low-grade labor.

This would make more pleasant reading if it were science fiction. As it is, the idea of man-animal chimeras is shocking and frightening.

When I was planning these chapters on the biological revolution, I debated with myself whether or not to include these most "far out" predictions about cloned people, deliberate mutations, cyborgs, and chimeras. Anyone is shocked when he first hears of these incredible predictions about the future. Some readers may be so shocked that they will close their minds to the whole biological revolution. This would be understandable. But it would be tragic. However unpleasant these ideas may be, society must face up to them.

So I have included these shocking ideas hoping to show how far the plans of some scientists have progressed. When apparently intelligent men start talking seriously about mixing men and animals, people need to wake up and find out what is going on.

These bizarre predictions raise some basic questions: What is man? What are the unique, unchanging qualities of human life with which men should not tamper?

As Paul Ramsey points out, what is at stake is not Christianity, but humanity. He sees these techniques as forms of species suicide. If they are adopted on a wide scale, they will dehumanize and destroy man.

It is no coincidence that these kinds of man-made men cause so many people to think immediately of Mary Shelley's classic story. Her scientist tried to create a living being of a human type—a humanoid. But the very name of the scientist became identified with the monster he created—*Frankenstein!*

At the very heart of the problem is the question, What is man? Most of the scientists on the frontier of the biological revolution seem to have the same answer to this basic question. They believe that man is a machine. A complex machine. A sophisticated machine. A biological machine. But still a machine.

Donald Fleming, a historian at Harvard, observes that "the biological revolutionaries of today are not antireligious but simply unreligious." [3] They believe that modern man is living in a post-Christian age in which Christian values and teachings are irrelevant.

This insight helps explain many things about the kinds of proposals they are making. They consider it their mission to seek to improve this complex machine called man. Therefore, they are willing to run the "moral" risk of experimenting with living human tissue. Of creating men outside marriage and the family. Of creating strange mutations, cyborgs, and chimeras. In short, of remaking humanity in a new image.

The biological revolutionaries do not consider these to be moral issues. They do not believe that the new age should be bound by existing moral rules. Instead, they believe that the moral values of the new age should grow out of the situations that arise in the new post-Christian age.

By contrast, Christians see man as a unique creation of God, a person of worth—capable of relating to God and man. Thus, man is more than a physical-chemical machine. Man obviously *involves* physical and chemical mechanisms, but man *is* not such a mechanism. Man is much more than a mechanism. He is a moral and spiritual personality created by God.

Therefore, Christians struggle with the moral problems created by the biological revolution. Paul Ramsey identifies two very different attitudes toward the ethical problems. One man assumes that we must do whatever science makes possible. Then ethics can be redefined to fit the new situation. "In contrast, a man of serious conscience means to say in raising urgent ethical questions that there may be some things men should never do." [4]

The Christian does not believe that man should become a helpless pawn of his own scientific discoveries. That science can create man-made men does not necessarily indicate that society *should* proceed with such a process.

A generation ago, science discovered how to make a nuclear bomb. But since 1945, society has recognized the dangerous consequences of using such bombs. Should not the same principle be applied to the explosive possibilities of the biological revolution?

At the very least, society needs to be aware of the biological revolution. Decisions of any kind must be based on facts, not fears. Scientists sometimes have withheld information from the public. This has been done either from preoccupation with their work or from fear of public interference with their work.

However, withholding information is dangerous for all concerned. Gordon Rattray Taylor reminds scientists that the public image of the scientist in the Middle Ages was that of a mad engineer. Then the medical advances of the nineteenth and twentieth centuries changed the image to that of a benevolent man in a white coat. Taylor warns that unless something is done the former image may return: "As the impact of the biological time-bomb begins to be felt, the haunted look of Dr. Frankenstein may gradually appear on the faces of biologists." [5]

The sharing of information should lead to planning and decision-making by responsible elements in society. Many people are aware of the need for some kind of control.

In the past, society often has failed to plan how to cope with other kinds of scientific and technological advances. For example, no plans were made for the industrial revolution of the eighteenth century. Among the results were uprooted families, disease-ridden slums, and terrible working conditions. The current environmental crisis is another example of what happens when science and technology advance without careful planning for moral and social consequences.

We cannot afford to make the same mistake in the coming biological revolution. If we do nothing, Taylor predicts that the result will be biological slums which cause more misery and death than the disease-ridden slums of the industrial revolution.

Salvador Luria, biologist at Massachusetts Institute of Technology, is one of the scientists who is calling for planning. As a scientist, he opposes the idea of a moratorium on science. He writes: "What is needed, rather, is a rational machinery, both national and international, to determine sensible policies and priorities in the application of scientific knowledge." [6]

Any such responsible planning should have a broad base of representation—government, science, education, and religion. Some people may balk at the idea of including religion. Strangely enough, these objections come from two very different groups. One group is made up of unbelievers. They believe that religion is irrelevant. The other group is made up of believers. Some of them think that such issues should not be the business of Christians and churches.

Leroy Augenstein is a Christian as well as a scientist. He makes a strong plea for religious people to speak out on these issues. He points out that the church and the home have been vital influences in the past. He acknowledges that the influence of both has waned. But Augenstein hopes that both home and church will exert their rightful influence as society faces the coming biological revolution.

Christians have a responsibility to become informed about the issues of the biological revolution. And they have a responsibility to exert what influence they can. Science and society need the moral conviction and spiritual insight of Christians. This need will increase, not decrease, as the biological revolution becomes a reality.

---

[1] *Science Digest* (November, 1969), pp. 6–13.

[2] Quoted by R. Michael Davidson, "Living in a Biological Revolution," *Current* (March, 1969), p. 8.

[3] Donald Fleming, "On Living in a Biological Revolution," *The Atlantic Monthly* (February, 1969), p. 67.

[4] Paul Ramsey, *Fabricated Man: The Ethics of Genetic Control* (New Haven: Yale University Press, 1970), p. 123.

[5] Gordon Rattray Taylor, *The Biological Time Bomb* (New York: The New American Library, Inc., 1968), p. 220.

[6] S. E. Luria, "Modern Biology: A Terrifying Power," *Nation* (October 20, 1969), p. 408.

9

65 Is a Lousy Age
Bill Stephens

Youth owned the 60's. Senior citizens will own the 70's. As turbulent as was the last decade, the 70's will be more life changing. At age 65 most men are too old to start new careers and too young to stop working. That fact already is shaping your future.

• The trend in industry is toward lowering the retirement age. The UAW in 1972 successfully won their "30-and-out" demand. Any employee with thirty years or more service may retire at age 56. In other industries early retirement pressure comes from the top down. Numerous companies want employees to opt for early retirement, even at age 55, and offer bonus incentives to get them to do so. The rationale primarily is economic, but the trend is set nonetheless.

• Growing disenchantment with materialistic goals is not limited to youth. The changing emphasis on community service efforts and plain joy in living will provide a better mental climate, so that retirees will not feel put on the shelf. A retiree's own attitude toward himself is much of the cause of his rapid decline of health, according to the AMA.

• Growing political muscle of retirees will result in laws geared to their needs. The National Council of Senior Citizens (now 2½ million strong) helped push through Medicare. Other senior citizens are organizing in groups, both political and nonpolitical, like the American Association of Retired Persons (2 million members) and the new Gray Panthers. Senior citizens control 15 percent of the votes in America, and their turnout record is higher than any other age.

• New studies are breaking down the old myths about growing old.

• With the life expectancy increasing and the population growth decreasing, senior citizens are becoming a larger percentage of the U.S. population. Moreover, during the last decade the number of persons aged 75 and over increased three times as fast as those from age 65 to 74. Even now, 13,000 Americans are over 100 years of age. Prospects both for increasing longevity and for increasing health during old age are bright.

Today, 20 million Americans are aged 65 or over. That's ten percent of the population. Every 20 seconds, another American reaches that watershed age.

But should 65 be the watershed age?

Back in 1882, Chancellor Bismarck of Germany established 65 as the retirement age for those he called "soldiers of labor." During the Depression in the U.S., Bismarck's model was adopted to create more jobs for younger men. The world was different back then. In 1930 only 6,649,000 persons were age 65 or over (5.4 percent of the population). Now, about the same number of persons are age 76 or older as were age 65 or older in 1930. A 65-year-old man in relatively good health is not old; and by 1930 standards, he won't be for another ten or fifteen years.

No one knows for sure what happens to make people grow old, but a number of theories are now being tested. The DNA molecule (nature's building block) figures in some of the theories. Dr. Augustus B. Kinzel of Salk Institute of Biological Studies told the Senate's 1967 Special Committee on Aging that we can expect "control of the aging process to provide the health and vigor necessary to that productivity in the span of 65 to 75 in which now we have in the span of 45 to 55 years of age."

Other theories are nongenetic. One holds that immunity to disease breaks down with age. Some laboratory tests indicate that the breakdown may be controlled by mixing young cells with old ones to restore the antibody-producing ability of older cells.

Though increasing vigor of the elderly already is apparent, we still live under the views of yesteryear. The picture—so favored by media—of an old, emaciated woman sitting forlornly on a rickety rocking chair on the porch of a dilapidated house is not an accurate picture of old age. Only four percent of the elderly live in institutions of any kind; only one percent are in mental hospitals (and half of them were confined while young). Only another two to three percent are bedfast at home. In fact, the majority of old people under age 75 are active.

Numerous studies are exploding the myths about old age. Previous studies had the elderly coming off badly when compared to the young people. However, social scientists now insist that the tests were designed for youngsters, not older people. Duke University Center for the Study of Aging and Human Development has determined by tests that the elderly can memorize and recall information quite well when compared to younger people, though they need more time to do it. Moreover, tests indicate that age does not have so much to do with slowness as *attitude* of the elderly toward themselves—primarily their fear of failure.

Other tests indicate that:

☆ level of education determines scores on tests to a far greater extent than does age;

☆ students are more senile than their elders;

☆ decrease in intelligence is linked to high blood pressure, not to the aging process itself;

☆ in areas where experience is influential (general information, vocabulary), intelligence goes up with age;

☆ creative productivity remains high in fields like mathematics, invention, botany, the humanities, statesmanship, logic, and philosophy;

☆ the older generation is more liberal than the younger generation;

☆ the work attendance record of older workers is some 20 percent better than younger workers, and the oldsters have only about half as many acute illnesses per year (though recuperation takes longer).

History abounds with examples of vigorous productivity in old age: Winston Churchill was Prime Minister of Great Britain at 81; W. Somerset Maugham wrote into his 80's; Toscanini still conducted the National Broadcasting System Orchestra at 87; Pablo Casals still plays cello at age 96; George Bernard Shaw wrote some of his most important works in his 70's; John Wesley was still preaching at 88; Frank Lloyd Wright designed the Guggenheim Museum at 86.

Carl Yung insisted that a person should continue to develop inwardly through the aging process. He lived what he preached until age 85.

If all of this is true, why then do so many persons die shortly after retirement?

In a letter introduced as testimony before the Committee on Aging mentioned above, Dr. F. J. L. Blasingame wrote for the American Medical Association:

"As physicians, we have seen too often the negative effect which such arbitrary denial of work opportunities can have on the health of older people.

"The AMA has been on record for a number of years as urging the exploration and adoption of flexible retirement policies based on individual ability and desire to continue working . . .

". . . Considerable medical evidence is available to indicate that the sudden cessation of productive work and earning power of an individual, caused by compulsory retirement at the chronological age of 65, often leads to physical and emotional illness and premature death."

According to Dr. Lester Carr, a psychologist, the five years following retirement comprise a period of low morale. Current practices, then, are unintentionally killing off the population soon after retirement.

But there is another side to the coin. Many persons *do* look backward as they grow older. Management can become archaic. Businesses often retire or reshuffle management personnel to get a stodgy business moving again. Generation gaps can develop. Social conscious young Turks in business can fight pitched battles against old liners who are convinced that profit ultimately is the only function of management.

Robert Kastenbaum reported results of his study *(Psychology Today,* Dec. '71) that during early adulthood a person begins the process of looking backward. By age 40, most persons are past-oriented; by age 55, virtually all persons are.

Aging, however, may have little to do with the backward look. Peter Drucker, in *The Age of Discontinuity,* insists that "people cannot stand a working life of fifty years. It is simply too long for them." A few pages later he continues: "a good many knowledge workers [persons whose work is based on knowledge rather than manual skill] tend to tire of their jobs in early middle age. Long before they reach retirement age, let alone long before they become physically and mentally disabled, the sparkle, the challenge, the excitement have gone out of their work."

Kastenbaum's studies support Drucker's assertion. He found that the attitude of younger workers toward older employees (especially the practice of politely ignoring the older person's advice) is a chief cause of the backward look.

Most sociologists point to three periods of life—study (one quarter), work (one half), and retirement (one quarter). But the periods of life do not need to remain forever in that order.

Knowledge is accumulated, and society develops at such a rapid pace today that most people make their contributions to a given field by their mid-forties. *Yet when a person enters a new career, his creativity is renewed.*

The military services long have followed policies that retire most career men and women by age 55. Many of the retirees go into second careers and do quite well. Their experience indicates the quality of contribution that may be made by a second-career person who has ceased to function creatively in his first career.

The second career idea is the first of several proposed alternatives to restructure the three-phase life cycle.

• The second career alternative has the weight of test results to indicate its workability. Career choices generally are made in youth, when so few options are known. For those who made choices they would not have made had more information been available, a second career allows them to break down the fences and open life up again. But more, new careers continually develop that were nonexistent a few years before. The second career plan allows a person to enter such new fields, so that his life experience can bring added dimensions to the new field.

The chief concrete problem that exists in pursuing a second career is financial. How does a middle-aged worker, perhaps with kids in college, maintain an acceptable standard of living while in training?

☆ The early retirement trend in industry will provide a livelihood, enabling some persons to train for a second career.

☆ Limited efforts already are in effect to grant up to two years college credit based on experience (testing is required). The clamor is growing for more liberal academic recognition of experience.

☆ Proposals have been made already for the government to fund training for second careers, either by loan guarantees or outright stipends. It is argued that the public will save on social security costs even if outright grants are made, because people will stay in the work force longer.

The bigger problem may be abstract—that of attitude. Changes must come about in attitudes toward the senior years, toward the meaning of vocation, toward the place of government in funding for such training, and on the part of business toward employee loyalty and tenure.

The same problems exist when other alternatives are considered, for the second career is only one proposal toward making better use of the increasing life span. With any alternative, the use of leisure time must be considered. Since Americans consider income production to be the chief reason for expending their energy, attitudes toward use of time must change.

• The four-day work week is another alternative. Theoretically, the additional leisure time will accomplish several goals: Workers will not burn out on a job as soon; week-by-week production will increase; people will develop satisfying and creative ways to use their leisure time, thereby increasing their joy for living; and some gung-ho workers may pursue two careers side by side. A number of companies are on four-day work weeks, including Southern Baptists' Radio and Television Commission and Brotherhood Commission (both were on a trial basis last summer).

• Another alternative is sabbatical time off periodically during a career. For example, Xerox allows its employees who have three years service or more to take paid leaves to do social work. Xerox makes up the difference in pay to the level of the employee's salary, even up to one hundred percent of the amount. Begun last January, the program is too new to evaluate. Some institutions, especially educational, long have granted sabbaticals to employees for study, writing, or other efforts that relate to the employee's work. Xerox has no such restrictions.

• Some social scientists propose a study, work, and community service division of life. During the third phase, persons could work in such efforts as the old Peace Corps and VISTA. Several organizations make use of the talents of the retired. Operation Green Thumb hires retired farmers for landscaping and gardening. The International Executive Service Corps helps retired executives lend their management skills to developing countries. Foster Grandparents pays 4,000 or so low-income persons over age 60 to be "grandparents" to over 8,000 underprivileged and retarded children. The Oliver Wendell Holmes Association harnesses retired managers to meet critical problems such as environmental control, education, housing, and race relations. Southern Baptists' Foreign Mission

Board has a missionary associate program that has used a number of retirees to fill critical positions that not only utilized their distinctive skills but also released career missionaries for the work they feel called to do.

Efforts such as these could be increased significantly. The chief drawback to this alternative is that, so far, too few types of vocations are tapped. Nonetheless, this alternative can be implemented more easily than the others and may well serve as a stepping-stone while attitudes change as to what life is for.

Other proposed alternatives include:

• Reduce retirement age to 38. This proposal is based on the labor force necessary to produce the current gross national product. However, the GNP now is coming under heavy fire as a valid measurement of American economic life.

• Lengthen the time required for work preparation and subsidize education for young people. Today, though, some educators insist that education can be streamlined; that youth already defer entry into the labor market too long.

• Cut annual work time to six months. This proposal calls for rotating work forces, each group working for half a year. The pros and cons are similar to the four-day work week proposal.

As employees develop their retirement policies over the next few years, they should observe differences among people. A company should allow the employees as many alternatives as possible.

The AMA opposes retirement keyed to any specific age. Instead, the organization suggests that three fundamentals should operate: (1) the individual's desire to work; (2) his ability to work; (3) the employer's need for the skill or ability which the individual offers, or potentially can offer. The AMA proposes measurements periodically throughout life to determine whether an employee should be retrained, retired, or—in some cases—dismissed, with competent counseling during each period of measurement.

Competent counseling, in fact, can begin immediately. When John W. Gardner was Secretary of HEW, he called for mid-career clinics, sponsored by schools, unions, and other organizations, where men and women could evaluate their life goals and consider changes of direction. Mr. Gardner also called for preretirement counseling. Employers and others should begin talking with workers several years before retirement to help them prepare and/or choose alternatives.

The decade of the 70's will see life-changing developments in employment and retirement. Anything that has to do with life has to do with God. Christians should be at the forefront with moral insights.

And, by the way, we're talking about all of us.

Mercy Killing: Right or Wrong?
Bill Stephens

The Hippocratic oath states that doctors will (1) relieve suffering, and (2) prolong and protect life. Sometimes, though, the two goals come in sharp conflict. What should a doctor do then?

Mercy killing (euthanasia) has been proposed by various moralists and practiced by various societies at least as long as history has been recorded. Generally, though, Christian spokesmen through the centuries have frowned on euthanasia. The reasons for their opposition are complex, ranging from belief that only God can take a life to the need for consciousness when the sacrament of extreme unction is administered.

Euthanasia is proposed more often now, and frequently by Christians, because science has become so proficient at keeping a patient's body alive even after he is dead in every other way.

"When is a person dead?" is a highly debated question. The answer is not even certain in legal circles. The body often does not die all at once, but in a lingering way. Vital functions may cease long before the heart stops beating. Or the heart may stop beating (and can be resuscitated) while the brain continues to function. More and more, the test of death is whether the brain has ceased to function. At that point, a person may be considered dead theologically and socially, even if some of the organs continue to perform.

The uncertainty has led to a serious consideration of what constitutes life. A significant and widely held view among moralists is that life must be considered in terms of personhood. When a person totally loses the ability to relate to other persons (and, it is assumed, to God) he no longer is a person. He is dead, socially and theologically. Harmon L. Smith quotes from a 1968 World Medical Association document: "The time of death of various body cells and organs is less important than the determination that the process has become irreversible, irrespective of resuscitation techniques that may be employed" *(Ethics in the New Medicine,* Abingdon).

Essentially, this view is that a person should be allowed to die without prolonging his pain and ignominy by machine and medication. Actually, doctors frequently decide—with or without consulting the survivors—to allow patients to die. Sometimes death even is hastened by a physican. Though numerous such cases have come to trial, not a single doctor ever has been convicted in America for his action.

There are three other views of euthanasia: (1) A person should, with adequate safeguards, be allowed to die if he so chooses; (2) Seriously malformed or retarded persons should be euthanasized; (3) Persons who are a burden on the community should be euthanasized. A person may believe in one form of euthanasia without believing in the other forms.

It is this writer's opinion that the first view is open to discussion among Christians, while the last two are not. We simply are too infantile morally and scientifically to cope adequately with those alternatives. Further, the decision should not be made by one person, but talked out by members of various professions, including ministers and theologians.

Several arguments are proposed in favor of euthanasia: (1) Death is a process; its arrival cannot be pinpointed with precision. (2) We cannot abdicate responsibility to judge when death occurs. (3) Death is more than biological; it includes personhood. (4) We should show mercy in death as well as in life. (5) A lingering death drains a family emotionally and financially. (6) A lingering death costs in other lives because it uses up much-needed medical resources. (7) Refusal to allow death is a denial of the Christian view of eternity—that death is only a gate to a better life. (8) Euthanasia is not different from suicide to avoid torture. (9) Other evils, such as loss of personal integrity, are worse than death.

Arguments against euthanasia include: (1) All life is precious, and even the terminal patient has a right to live as long as possible. (2) An unsaved patient has a chance, however small, to be saved. (3) A cure for a dying person's disease might yet be found. (4) The patient's condition may have been misdiagnosed. (5) The legalization of euthanasia may destroy the doctor/patient relationship. (6) Voluntary euthanasia is suicide. (7) Involuntary euthanasia is murder. (8) Only God has the right to take a life. (9) Patients racked by pain might make a decision impulsively. (10) Legalization would weaken our moral fiber. (11) Legalization would weaken medical research and take away incentive to find cures. (12) Heirs might use euthanasia to hasten a death that is to their benefit. (13) Once legalized, the application of euthanasia would spread.

Some of the arguments, of course, cancel each other out. But, more importantly, some basic assumptions are in conflict. Those against euthanasia have the weaker arguments. They tend to have a concept of death that does not deal adequately with its realities; they tend to build their case on the exceptions; they tend to fear the results of euthanasia without adequate survey of historical parallels (capital punishment, martydom, war, current medical practices). Nevertheless, their cautions regarding the sanctity of life carry heavy weight in spite of their arguments.

The debate comes down to a matter of cases. Few people would object to a doctor's turning off a resuscitator to allow a slowly dying patient with irreversible brain damage to die. But where, beyond that case, is the line to be drawn? And few people cannot sympathize with a terminal cancer patient who, pain-racked and overwrought about the expense and drain his condition places on his family, refuses further treatment. But where, beyond that case, is suicide clearly *not* justified?

The lines cannot be drawn. We must learn to trust human judgment.

During the next half decade, our nation (and each state) will face some tough decisions about laws that deal with ethical issues. Euthanasia is only one issue in the medical field, each of which involves human drama.

Groups, both pro and con, have proposed various types of legislation on each issue. Every proposal can be picked to pieces. Every proposal has inherent dangers. But we must keep before our eyes like a phylactery the fact that what we are doing now (or not doing) isn't working too well, either.

The fact is that no law can be written that takes into account the human dynamics involved in such two-sided issues. However, laws can be drawn up that will protect life, liberty, and the pursuit of happiness by circumscribing the way decisions are arrived at. A state or nation may make one man in a community legally responsible for all decisions regarding euthanasia. That process would be efficient, but no one man has enough moral insight for such momentous power over life, death, and health.

In practice, though, this one-man power is what is operative today—and the one man is not appointed or elected by anyone. He is the family doctor. He may choose or not choose to pull the plug on a resuscitator, depending on his views on euthanasia, for example.

Henry A. Davidson, MD concludes in his chapter in *Should Doctors Play God?* (edited by Claude A. Frazier, MD, Broadman): "As a scientist I conclude that all logic is on the side of euthanasia. As a physician I will not take the power to put someone to death." He also argues that: "When the chips are down, this is a responsibility for the physician, not an item to be placed on the agenda of a conclave of relatives."

Dr. Davidson should not be coerced into performing euthanasia; but neither should his unwillingness decide the issue. No one profession—even one so related to life and death as medicine—has sufficient insight to dictate answers to the questions surrounding euthanasia. A doctor's training gives him biological insights, but moral insights do not necessarily follow. In fact, a doctor may have a built-in bias against death that may make him less able to render a moral decision than a competent minister or a loving relative. The decision should be a group process.

In 1971, Dr. Christian Barnard transplanted both a heart and a lung to Adrian Herbert. The donor's wife, in tears, revealed that she was not even aware of her husband's death before the organs were taken from his body; she certainly had not given her permission. Some of Barnard's colleagues strongly criticized him; some even accused him about outright experimentation. We do not impugn Dr. Barnard. But that controversy demonstrates what an impossible situation exists when such decisions are limited to the medical profession.

Any decision involving such life-ending or life-changing factors should be made by a group—a legally-controlled group. The medical profession should be represented, so should an appropriate religious representative be a part of the group, and so should the closest family member be involved. Perhaps a competent psychologist, too, should be part of the process. Taking into account all the factors involved (which necessarily calls into play each person's prejudices), a decision should be rendered *in terms of the persons immediately affected,* as well as the effect of the proposed action on society itself.

That kind of process scares most of us. And that is just the point. We don't trust ourselves any more to make ethical decisions. We prefer to hammer out a precisely-worded law that contains no loop holes, that prescribes certain actions in every conceivable situation, that eliminates every possible human error.

We are never going to get that kind of legislation. And so long as we try, in our customary unrealistic fashion, we will continue in effect our current practice of leaving ultimate decisions to one person in the medical profession. As a doctor friend told me:

"Some doctors are more gutsy than others." Who wants such decisions to rest on how gutsy his doctor might happen to be?

So: Let's bring trust in human judgment back into vogue—collective human judgment, by competent persons, circumscribe the bylaw. Mistakes will be made, but not so many as now.

This writer believes that laws should be drafted to allow euthanasia in extreme cases of terminal illness, at the patient's request if he is conscious, by those closest to him if he is not, the action to be carefully circumscribed by legal certification and by involving several professional people in the decision. The practice of euthanasia should not be extended to infants (beyond current practices), nor to persons—under any conditions—who may be considered burdens to the community.

II

Cremation: Is It Christian?
D. P. Brooks

Ancient Babylon considered the peace of departed spirits to be dependent upon proper burial. In Persia, the bodies were exposed to birds of prey so that dirt or fire would not defile the holy elements. The Greeks believed that cremation speeded the spirit on its way, hurrying the liberation of spirit from body. Even the Hebrews felt that the fate of the departed was affected by the disposal of the body. Societies have disposed of their dead in six basic ways: (1) earth burial, (2) cremation, (3) conservation (embalming, as in Egypt), (4) exposure to the elements, (5) animal consumption, and (6) water burial. One of the major factors in methods of disposal has been religious beliefs. For example, the Egyptian practice of embalming and preserving the corpse was related to their beliefs regarding the future life of the departed in another existence. Fear of the dead caused most ancient societies to exercise great care in disposing of dead bodies.

The practice of cremating the dead goes back to the period near the end of the Bronze Age. Both the Greeks and the Romans practiced cremation, and so did the people in what is now Germany, France, and England.

The Romans built their funeral pyres in the form of an altar. As the flames leapt up, an eagle was sometimes released to soar high into the sky, symbolizing the flight of the soul. With the Roman people, as with other ancient societies, the funeral rites were passage rites, sending the soul on its way to its final destination.

The Hebrews abhorred cremation and preferred earth burial. Failure to be buried was a disgrace and was forbidden by the law (see Lev. 20:14; 21:9; Josh. 7:25). The Hebrews sometimes left graves open to speed up disintegration of the fleshly part of the body; then the bones were buried. The burning of the body before the bones were consumed was looked upon with horror. Amos pronounced the judgment of God on the Edomites because they "burned the bones of the king of Edom into lime" (Amos 2:1). Such destruction of the bones was considered an abomination because it disturbed the spirit of the departed dead and, consquently, could bring down wrath on the guilty party.

For the first few centuries after Christ, funerals among the Christians were a joyous affair as they celebrated the hope of eternal life. However, by the eighth century funerals had taken on a solemn and sorrowful tone, primarily because of a particular emphasis on the Christian doctrine of bodily resurrection and an expectation of the early return of Christ. According to popular belief, the destruction of the corpse by fire was a desecration of the former temple of the Holy Spirit. Also, since the body was soon to be raised, people feared that the destruction of the body would interfere with the new life. Thus, the widespread use of cremation in Europe was, until modern times, replaced by earth burial.

Some funerals today have recovered some of the hope and confidence reflected by the early Christians. Since we do not know when Christ will return, we have to make plans on the basis that life on earth may continue for generations to come—barring ecological catastrophe or nuclear war. In view of the total dissolution of the body over a period of centuries, believers today probably have less fear regarding the body than did early Christians. For both of these reasons, this generation of Christians probably will not look upon cremation as a threat to future life or as in any way antagonistic to the faith.

Paul said that "flesh and blood cannot inherit the kingdom of God" (1 Cor. 15:50). Paul said, again, that the body "is sown a natural body; it is raised a spiritual body" (1 Cor. 15:44). Perhaps modern man, better than his ancestors, can picture a future life in which personality survives death independent of an earthly body. Whatever form eternal life takes, modern believers seem indisposed to make it dependent on the material elements of an earthly body. Paul said that God would give a body suitable to the life in eternity (see 1 Cor. 15:35–44). Bodies return to the earth eventually, whatever dissolution is rapid or slow. The rate of dissolution does not seem to be important in relation to the new life God provides for his own: "As we have borne the image of the man of dust, we shall also bear the image of the man from heaven" (1 Cor. 15:45, RSV).

One of the factors that may have a bearing on the question of cremation is the threat of nuclear destruction. In case of atomic war, millions of people could be "cremated free and equal," as a wag expressed it. Could this in any way interfere with the destiny of the people of God? The question needs no answer. In view of the total decay of multitudes of believers' bodies and the possibilities of nuclear destruction, the concept of cremation as a threat to the future of the Christian dead seems largely academic.

The practice of cremating the dead has grown rapidly in the last generation, both in England and in this country. Its revival in modern times goes back to Sir Henry Thompson, who in 1874 organized the Cremation Society of England. He was concerned with the amount of space allotted to earth burial in a land that was already crowded. Furthermore, he realized the danger caused by infected water from the cemeteries. Against very intense opposition from the public and the churches, he tried to bring the light of reason and science to the question. He answered those who objected that the destruction of the body would interfere with the resurrection with another question: What about the sainted martyrs who were burned at the stake? Would they not fare as well in the resurrection as others? The question and answer convinced an increasing number of people that this concern is not valid.

The late George Bernard Shaw, famous writer and wit, was a strong advocate of cremation. He said: "Dead bodies can be cremated. All of them ought to be; for earth burial, a horrible practice, will some day be prohibited by law, not only because it is hideously unaesthetic, but because the dead would crowd the living off the earth if it could be carried out to its end." [1] The success of those who advocated this view is revealed in the fact that England today has over 160 crematoria and cremates over a third of all its dead. A former British pastor, now living in the U.S.A., reports that about four out of five of his funeral services during the last years of his pastorate in England involved cremation. Usually the earth burials involved older persons who owned burial lots and planned to be buried beside a deceased mate. He reported that hardly any of the younger families were investing in cemetery lots. Instead, they anticipate cremation. The remains are scattered or otherwise disposed of by the family.

One who drives by Mt. Sinai cemetery in New York City or by other huge cemeteries and considers the amount of space devoted to graves will inevitably ask whether man can continue to practice earth burial in our increasingly crowded metropolitan centers. In fact, there has been a 44 percent increase in cremation in the past decade in the U.S.A. The practice is much more common in certain sections of the nation than in others.

The increasing acceptance of cremation may be based on several factors besides religion and ecology: financial, legal, aesthetic, and emotional.

The funeral industry represents big business in the U.S.A. While it is difficult to determine the full costs of disposing of the dead, the United States Commerce Department estimated that the direct cost per funeral in the nation was about $1,000 in 1969—up from $675 in 1960. This means the average cost per funeral for every man, woman, child, and stillborn infant was $1,000. This figure includes the burial of indigents and prisoners who are buried by local and state governments at minimum expense. The statement of the Commerce Department added a note that "components of the entire funeral process seem to increase each year." [2]

One source indicated that one half of all florist sales go for funerals. This, added to the cost of shipping bodies for burial, drives costs up. Pre-need buying of cemetery and mausoleum space must be added. In light of the undernourished and poorly housed, plus the enormous needs in education and health care, serious questions are being raised regarding our stewardship of resources in disposing of the dead.

The author of a 300-page book on the subject estimated that when all expenses were included, Americans spent in 1960 about two billion dollars on the funeral industry. This compares with a total of 1.9 billion spent on the 3.6 million college and graduate school students in our colleges and universities. No one questions the obligation to provide appropriately for the reverent disposal of the bodies of loved ones, but who would want money spent unnecessarily on his funeral that could go to further his child or grandchild's education or welfare?

The funeral industry has shown keen interest in cremation and has weighed the possibility of its cutting into the income they now receive from earth burial. They have been successful in securing passage in some states of laws designed to protect their industry. For example, in most states a body must be embalmed, even though it is to be cremated quickly. In addition, a casket may be required. Further, a container for the remains may be required by law or by the funeral establishment.

One funeral company lists the following costs for cremation: A package deal is available for $475 that includes: casket (required by state law), pickup of body, a service in the chapel (if desired), and an urn for the remains. (The cost can be reduced if the body is not viewed during the service prior to cremation.) By comparison, interment costs include: casket (starting at $300), opening and closing grave ($175), lot ($250), vault (required by state law, $200). The amount totals $924, assuming that the least expensive casket is chosen, which probably isn't often the case. A group has organized in Dallas, Texas, to help its members through the cremation process for something like $50.00.

The legal question is raised when someone expresses a fear that cremation can be used as a cover for murder. Since the body is destroyed, no one can check later to discover whether foul play had been involved in the death. How can a society protect itself against such threats?

In England the practice of cremation is considered to be a protection against foul play because two licensed physicians have to sign the death certificate. The more careful check regarding the cause of death is seen as a means of detecting evidence of crime.

In Tennessee the death certificate of a body to be cremated must be signed by one physician. The crematorium in Nashville requires that the death statement be presented. Crematoria requires that the remains be placed in an urn. The one furnished by the funeral company is made of concrete covered with fiber glass and costs $75.00.

Even though cremation at first thought seems aesthetically questionable, in reality it has advantages. The aesthetic question is closely related to the emotions of the living toward the deceased loved one. Does cremation ease the hurt of separation from loved ones, or does it add to the grief? A pastor who has experienced both kinds of funerals has strong feelings on the subject. He believes that cremation is a far more desirable way of handling the funeral—from any viewpoint—and especially considering the feelings of the bereaved family. He sees the quick removal of the body as a help in accepting the finality of death of the loved one. Also, the simple disposal of ashes avoids the necessity of having elderly people stand out in rain, sleet, or snow while a body is committed to the earth. In addition, the pastor is in better position in a chapel to minister comfort to the family than when standing out in the open.

A visit to a local crematorium brought out some interesting

facts. This facility is only three years old and is the first in Tennessee. Previously the nearest crematorium was located at Louisville, Kentucky. An employee indicated that he could not identify any particular type of person who chooses cremation over earth burial. He did indicate that the families choosing cremation seemed less emotional than the average family group. He indicated that the sense of finality seems greater among families choosing cremation.

Custom is strong in matters concerning funerals and the disposal of the bodies of family members. Radical changes may be greeted with shock at first. Yet if a quick and clean disposal of the remains proves to ease the pain of yielding up the loved one's body to return to the elements, then a rapid shift of custom could occur.

In the cremation itself, a gas furnace is used. The body is placed in the oven and the heat is left on for two and a half hours. Then a waiting period of eight hours allows the oven to cool down sufficiently for the remains to be removed. Only the bone structure is left, and it is easily pulverized and placed in an urn.

The urn is given to the family and can be disposed of in any way it may wish. Some have the remains scattered from a plane, strewn in a wooded area or garden, or scattered on a beach. In case the family wants the urn buried in a cemetery plot owned by the funeral agency, the lots are available. To protect their investment, one Tennessee company will bury only two urns, about eight inches in diameter, in one cemetery plot. The company is building a twenty-story mausoleum in which niches will be provided for the urns that will contain human remains. At the present time, most families take the urns with them, and no questions are asked regarding their disposal.

One question that inevitably arises concerns the possibility of contamination from the remains. The answer is that absolutely no possibility of contamination exists.

Several conclusions emerged from the study of this theme. One is that the practice is growing most rapidly in countries where Christianity formerly had stopped cremation. The Roman Catholic

Church removed its ban against cremation in 1963. The practice is growing in Europe, the U.S.A., Australia, and New Zealand —countries where Christianity is the major religion. With increasing concern for ecology, everything points to a rapid increase in the practice of cremation among societies in which Christianity is predominant.

A second tentative conclusion is that this method of disposing of the remains of loved ones is more aesthetically acceptable than earth burial. Horror at the fact of death, yet love for the departed, combine to generate anxiety and sorrow. The committal of the body to a grave seems to be a particularly difficult experience.

In England the government will cremate a body for ten dollars. The English people who come to this country are shocked by the high cost of our funerals. The large amount of money being expended in this nation for the burial of bodies and the maintenance of cemeteries seems to some persons irresponsible if not pagan. Surely a better, more economical, more sensible, and more Christian way can be found to dispose of human bodies. Everything points to cremation as an increasingly acceptable part of change in funeral customs.

Christian doctrine was a major factor in stopping the custom of cremation in the western world for several centuries. Perhaps it is appropriate now that Christian nations are restoring it to a position of acceptance if not preference.

---

[1]Jessica Mitford, *The American Way of Death* (New York: Simon and Schuster, 1963), pp. 162–63.
[2]*The New York Times Encyclopedia Almanac 1972,* p. 495.

12

Let's Stop Political Pollution!
Bill Stephens

"Let's Stop Political Pollution!" What a slogan! Listen to the drums, the bugles, the tramp of feet. Watch the trombones swing back and forth. With flags flying, pipes piping, and crowds chanting, the parade of good guys has evil on the run.

A guy with a microphone waits at the parade's terminating point so he can ask the marchers what they plan to do besides march. Here they come. He smiles. The marchers look a little polluted themselves.

The microphone catches a middle-aged man by the arm to ask him the big question. "Put every crooked politician behind bars," he storms.

Sure, the microphone wonders, *and who would run the country?*

Here's one beaming face. Stop him. "How are you going to stop political pollution?" The beam grew beamier. "Why, by winning everyone to Christ."

Well, that sure will help, the guy with the microphone thought, *but what then? I knew a Christian once who was part of the political pollution problem.*

And so the interview went on into the loud, celebrating night. One sentence answers. But the microphone guy had covered parades like this one before. Most of the people, he knew, would disappear into the woodwork to wait for another parade. Some of them would vote, of course—"I don't like either one, but Jones is the lesser of two evils."

A call for repentance needs to be written into any article on how to stop political pollution. Politics is a microcosm of America. One way to stop political pollution is to change Americans. But that's not the only way. Our founding fathers were pretty cagey guys. They had an idea that Americans never would be perfect, so they built into the American process a system of checks and balances. Some historians even believe that those gentle giants posed one man's bad nature over against another's. American government would work because men would protect their self-interests. (Madison said: "Ambition must be made to counteract ambition.")

We should be so smart.

To stop political pollution, then, we should mix—as best we can—idealism with realism. We can be realistic about human nature and fight for laws that will regulate, or at least channel, avarice and self-seeking. We can select reasonably honest men, get them to run for office, then help them get elected. Three big steps must be taken in order to stop political pollution. The first two steps identify problem areas in preparation for step 3.

STEP ONE

IDENTIFY THE AREAS OF CORRUPTION.

☆ Campaign funding is a frequently mentioned and critical area. A bill now in effect limits the amount a candidate campaigning for national office may spend. Like most laws that seek to regulate ethics, enterprising souls will find loopholes. Nevertheless, the new law closed most of the loopholes of the old 1925 Federal Corrupt Practices Act.

A truly satisfactory solution, though, will not exist until the money problem of seeking office is solved. The facts of life are progressive: It takes money to get elected; a candidate must find the money somewhere; and most candidates will accept money from special interest groups when the only alternative is to stop running.

☆ Invective is a second area of corruption. Until editorials in church papers around the country alerted voters to the plan, some politicians began a "billboarding" smear campaign—in which candidates erect billboards accusing their opponents of voting against prayer in the schools. That's invective. Writing off opponents of busing as racists is invective, too; and so is writing off those Americans who lean to the left as "an effete corps of impudent snobs." Invective comes from all parts of the political spectrum.

☆ Interest groups comprise a third area. In a broad sense, an interest group is a band of people organized to get something done. Oil lobbies, the American Dairy Association, highway interests, and ITT are some of the interest groups that have been in the news lately. But: a church-related college that seeks to influence the state to purchase land for another legitimate purpose, a group of Christians who organize to defeat a liquor bill, and the Baptist Joint Committee on Public Affairs all are special interest groups.

The politics of democracy could not exist without interest groups. They are essential channels for expression of the will of the people. The *democratic value* of an interest group lies not in its ability to exercise power, though, but to the extent that it represents people. Generally speaking, the most powerful groups are that way because of money, not because they represent a group of Americans. Thus, a vital link between the people and government is blocked because money can provide good lobbyists, top legal counsel, and other influences on lawmakers that have little to do with a number of people the group represents.

Additionally, the more money a person has, the more special interest groups he can join. A migrant grape picker does well to find enough time for his labor group. A well-paid businessman, however, can join several groups and—because of his knowhow and connections—can influence all of them.

These three areas are not the only ones that need unpolluting. But they represent perhaps the most glaring areas, and at least demonstrate the complexity of the struggle. That struggle is further complicated by tensions and dynamics that exist now in our country.

STEP TWO

IDENTIFY THE TENSIONS WITHIN SOCIETY.

The tensions and dynamics at work in the United States overlap and intermesh in a fashion so complicated that separate identification tends to oversimplify. Nevertheless, such a process gives some idea of what we are in for. The tensions indicate areas of life in which corruption needs to be challenged; and an evaluation of the tensions emphasizes that the quality of the society is reflected in its government.

At least four areas of tension may be identified:

☆ Challenge to business is obvious in: anger of consumers over rising prices and over shoddy or unfairly advertised products; anger of workers when pension funds can't deliver as promised; legal challenge to credit practices; and the public's fear of growing financial muscle of conglomerates.

☆ The rising cost of living has become a significant campaign issue. The common man cannot help but suspect that if economists promote conflicting theories, the problem is bigger than any of them. Although greed has something to do with rising prices, the problem cannot be written off simply as corruption. Better understanding of the dynamics of international economy and policies based on that understanding is likely the most important solution for this problem.

☆ The responsibility of business for shoddy merchandise, built-in obsolescence, and untruthful advertising is another matter. Ralph Nader, Common Cause, the FDA, and other forces are applying considerable pressure on business to reform. Inside business itself, the battle rages. Oldliners insist that the purpose of management is to make a profit. Period. Morality is the purview of the stockholders. They should decide, if anyone should, what is ethical and what is not. Young Turks, on the other hand, insist that management is morally responsible for whatever happens because of its decisions and policies.

This conflict is more important than it sounds. It is, in fact, a wave of the future. The results will affect consumers and politics more significantly perhaps than any other movement. Ecology is involved, and so is quality of goods and labor practices. But in terms of political pollution, the results could well change the nature of lobbying pressure on legislators.

☆ Pension funds are under scrutiny. The worker often is maneuvered out of the pension he has worked toward for many years—sometimes because the fund is improperly managed, sometimes because the company goes bankrupt, sometimes because the company retires or lays him off when he is too old to build retirement elsewhere, and often because he changes jobs and loses his benefits.

Several bills have been proposed to regulate pension funds. Especially as society becomes more mobile, workers find themselves losing their benefits. One reason for pension funds, of course, is to hold an employee's loyalty. However, employees often change for legitimate reasons and do not feel they should be restricted from moving to a better job or healthier climate because of a pension plan. Look for this debate to grow more intense during this next legislative term.

☆ Credit practices already have come under government scrutiny. Some regulations have been imposed on companies who operate under interstate commerce laws. However, even those corporations have convinced the courts to honor the distinction between "interest" and "carrying charges." The latter charge generally is much higher than allowable interest rates. State regulations especially are in need of reform, but special interest groups lobby quite successfully for loopholes within the law.

☆ Regulation of conglomerates is a critical challenge to business. Concern was loudly expressed through news media when oil companies moved in to monopolize sources of energy such as coal. The acquistions preceded an increase in utility cost for consumers. The ITT affair, whatever its political implications, is a case in point of a powerful, far-reaching conglomerate.

Around the turn of the century, several businessmen built such vast financial empires that they virtually ran the country, influencing both foreign and domestic policy. Teddy Roosevelt's trust-busting efforts diluted that strength, but today, through conglomerates, the focus of power in the hands of a few boards approaches that turn-of-the-century critical level.

Any corporation—conglomerate or otherwise—whose decisions affect virtually every man, woman, and child in America must be regulated. Giving human nature to be what it is, that kind of power guarantees corruption in government.

☆ Another area of tension might be called concern about quality of life. This dynamic puts pressure on education, institutions, environmental interests, society's goals, and personal freedom.

☆ Quality of education was vigorously attacked during the close of the sixties. Students insisted that education prepares them to make money, but does not prepare them to live happily. Much of education, some insisted, was irrelevant to life.

In their cries of distress, the students really said little that old-timers have not been saying for years: "You can't get it all from books."

The insistence on relevancy opened up new areas of inquiry to historians (black studies is a well-known example), and gained new practical courses as mundane as auto troubleshooting.

But students are not the only Americans hollering for a change. Since life expectancy has increased, men in their forties and fifties seek to enter new vocations. They insist that college credits should be given for their experience gained over the years. Some of them even insist that benefits to business will be considerable if some provision is made for men and women to enter second vocations later in life.

Educators themselves are divided; many of them agree that the years of preparation are too many. Courses of study, some insist, can be trimmed down so young men and women can get to work two to four years sooner. (There is a flip side to that record.)

☆ Authoritarian structures, including schools, are under heavy tensions. Churches (some less authoritarian than others), government agencies, and businesses all are challenged.

Essentially, the conflict lies in the tension between the rights of the individual and those of the institution. How much individual freedom should a person be required to give up for the orderly running of an institution? Examples: How much should a corporation be allowed to control an employee's life? To what degree should a school control dress habits of students? How much should public morality control private morality?

But an individual's rights include more than personal freedom *per se*. His creativity and competence are involved. In business, government, and education, why should incompetent persons continue to occupy powerful positions just because they have seniority? Conversely, why should a competent man or woman be forced to retire just because he reaches the arbitrarily-set age of sixty-five?

Alvin Toffler points out rather forcefully in *Future Shock* that employees look less and less to their bosses for approval; that they are prone to give their loyalty to a task rather than to an employer. Peter Drucker insists that an employee's first loyalty is to himself, not to his employer. These influences understandably create tension toward institutions.

This spirit of individual freedom is pretty Baptistic, but the developments have been diverse. The disenchantment with material goals has created significant tensions within families and corporations, and has spilled over into government. That spirit also has given rise to a concept of private morality that insists an individual has the right to do whatever he pleases in private. The assumption is that private morality has little to do with society itself. In spite of that assumption, private morality has quite a bit to do with corruption or the lack of it in government.

The Women's Liberation Movement is part of that spirit. The development will influence legislation significantly. Also, the growing competence of women due to training and experience enlarges the reservoir for good legislators.

The broad concerns of ecology relate to quality of life, of course. Concern for the environment may come under the quality of life heading, but ecological concerns permeate the whole fabric of society. As concern grows into hard action, lobbyists who advocate poor ecological policies and legislators who give in to such lobby pressures will be more and more on the defensive.

☆ Another tension America faces is the rise of citizen-oriented power groups. The development may have been propelled by the deterioration of urban living and ghetto unrest; but the rise probably was inevitable anyway, and likely had its roots in the unrest that led blacks and other minorities to leave their homes for the city in the first place.

But racial minorities constitute only a fraction of the power group picture. There are consumer interest groups, advocates of abortion reform, lobbyists for education, ecology groups, and women's rights groups, to name a few. Citizens fast are learning how to organize and influence legislation. The development has exciting implications for democracy, but also increases the danger of a fractured society.

☆ A reconsideration of U.S. goals, domestic and foreign, is another tension. What kind of leadership should the U.S. exert on the world scene? To what domestic needs should the U.S. direct its resources?

Tragically, these tensions exist alongside the three areas of corruption at a time when Americans demonstrate disenchantment with the government's ability to perform. The conviction is widespread through the citizenry that no one in Washington understands or cares about its problems, that the big money always wins, that politics is corrupt through and through.

Scientists claim that if a problem can be identified, it can be solved. Hopefully, then, this resumé of corruptions and tensions in the U.S. may be a starting place for you, a Christian, to identify the problems. You are left with the twofold task of pinpointing the corruption that exists within the tensions listed, and of finding areas of strength within those tensions that will help you work toward eliminating corruption.

Once a problem is identified, a solution may be mapped. Two cautions are in order: Christians should consider carefully that corruptions and tensions on the one hand, and government and society on the other, are interrelated; and Christians should develop long-range goals. Short-term solutions might at first bring cheering in the streets, but they will become corrupting influences themselves (as was the outcome of much simplistic legislation during the sixties).

STEP THREE

GET BUSY.

With those two cautions, ten steps might be followed toward solving the political pollution problem.

1. *Decide on a goal.* When you make a list of battles that need to be fought in politics, you can become pretty discouraged. You will discover numerous circumstances, laws, or practices that justly make your blood boil. If you are to effect a solution, though, you must establish one or two issues as priority goals to work toward; then trust other Christians to take care of the other needs.

2. *Organize or join a compatible group.* Emphasis must be placed on "compatible." An already-organized group may have a goal similar to yours, but its methods of attaining the goal may be distinctly unchristian. As a Christian, you should not—even at the risk of failure—fight God's battles with the devil's methods. Nor, however, should you be unnecessarily rigid. Size is potential strength.

If a group through which you can work toward your goal is not organized already, you may consider organizing one. One process is:

First, form a nucleus of several people, perhaps beginning with a friend or two.

Next, discuss the problem at length, identify a goal you want to reach, and determine a course of action. Goals include: getting an already-announced candidate into office (or convincing a likely person to run); employing legal counsel to pursue a matter through the courts; or building public sympathy toward changing or creating a law.

Then a broad base of popular support may be essential. In a small town, the phone book is a valid source of names for mail-outs and/or for telephone promotion. In a larger city, a book called *Kriss Kross* likely is available (for several dollars) that lists residents by street and number.

3. *Actively support a good candidate.* Volunteer workers are hard to come by for any candidate. If you are convinced that a candidate really is committed to your desired goal, you will be welcomed to his camp with open arms. But size him up well.

You are well within your rights as a potential worker (even as a voter) to expect a local candidate to talk with you personally. Listen to his answers carefully. Is he "talking to the gallery"? Does he only fain conviction? Even if he is sincere, you also should be convinced of his competence.

4. *Do not involve your church directly.* If you do, you will walk a fine line between Christian morality and partisanship. If you organize a group in your church, it should be approved by the entire church, and distinctive guidelines should be adopted. The group should recommend action to the church, which should then determine whether to take that action. The group should be forbidden by church policy to take action on its own. Its recommendations are by nature controversial, and such action is not central to a church's purpose, so this suggestion should be weighed carefully. *The church is responsible to vigorously encourage its members to be good citizens, but the church itself rarely should take a political stand.*

5. *Become thoroughly informed on an issue.* Be tough-minded.

Read arguments *against* as well as *for* your view. You may change your mind; it's happened before. You may become further convinced of your position, or you may temper your position and legitimately decide to work for a compromise. At any rate, you need to know the opposing arguments *as the opposition states them.* Otherwise, you will be annihilated in debate.

6. *Recognize the values and limitations of a resolution.* The value of a resolution has been debated. Barry Garrett built a pretty good case for them in *Report From the Capitol* (February, 1972). A Christian should not feel that he has performed his duties once his group has passed a resolution, though. Tough battles are not so simply won.

7. *Settle the party question.* Dan Grant, in *The Christian and Politics,* argues that a Christian exerts a stronger influence on politics through party loyalty than as an independent. That opinion should be carefully weighed. Other options are open to the voter, though, who cannot conscientiously commit himself to one party. Special interest groups as described above, and working for a particular candidate are two possibilities.

8. *Work.* Don't expect God to make the walls of Jericho fall. He might, but don't presume that he will. You can assume as axiomatic that you will have to work a lot harder to reach a Christian goal than an average person will to reach an unchristian or amoral goal.

9. *Be realistic.* Think long-range. Decide on an attainable goal. Don't dispel your commitment unrealistically. If your candidate can't win, or if your proposed bill hasn't a chance, decide on a goal you can accomplish. Perhaps you will decide to work toward the next election. Success isn't measured by dreams. Realism does not mean accepting substandard goals, but it does mean a short step is better than nothing.

10. *Vote intelligently.* While you can channel your efforts effectively only by limiting yourself to one or two goals, you can become informed on the wide range of issues. Then vote accordingly. As

you become familiar with other issues, you will learn the interrelatedness of American life. Thus you will gain insights that will help you work toward your goal.

How do you stop political pollution?

It ain't easy. But it's an American's job. And more, it's a Christian's job.

13

A New Case for an Old Conviction
Clyde Lee Herring

"And if all the combined forces of hell should assemble in conclave, and with them all the men of earth that hate and despise God, and purity, and virtue—if all the scum of the earth could mingle with the denizens of hell to try to think of the deadliest institution to home, to church and state, I tell you sir, the combined hellish intelligence could not conceive of or bring an institution that could touch the hem of the garment of the open licensed saloon to damn the home and manhood, and womanhood, and business, and every other good thing on God's earth." [1]

Forceful words, those! Billy Sunday was never a man to understate his convictions in colorful speech. His convictions about alcohol expressed the feeling of Baptists in the first quarter of the twentieth century.

But a new generation has arisen. Prohibition has been stricken from the law. It is estimated that 85 million adults—about 79 percent of all men and 63 percent of all women drink alcoholic beverages. Many are asking their ministers: "What does the Bible really teach about drinking? Does the Bible really teach total abstinence?"

Their questions are honest. They deserve honest answers. What, in fact, does the Bible teach about drinking?

The Bible, universally and without exception, prohibits drunkenness. Paul listed drunkenness with other forms of human wickedness: "Do you not know that the unrighteous will not inherit the kingdom of God? Do not be deceived; neither the im-

124

moral, nor idolaters, nor adulterers, nor homosexuals, nor theives, nor the greedy, nor drunkards, nor revilers, nor robbers will inherit the kingdom of God" (1 Cor. 6:9–10).[2]

Paul lists drunkenness with other vices as a part of the "works of the flesh" (Gal. 5:19). Solomon warns: "Be not among winebibbers or among gluttonous eaters of meat; for the drunkard and the glutton will come to poverty, and drowsiness will clothe a man with rags" (Prov. 23:20–21).

Nowhere does the Scripture approve drunkenness for whatever reason. It is universally condemned.

Again Solomon warns: "Wine is a mocker, strong drink a brawler; and whoever is led astray by it is not wise" (Prov. 20:1). But a nagging question remains to be answered for a person who is honest with the Word of God. Does the Bible prohibit moderate social drinking? What about those other passages? Don't they, in fact, seem to approve moderate drinking?

Here are some of the passages in the Bible that force the Christian to reexamine the case for total abstinence.

The same Solomon who warned against the dangers of drink advises: "Go, eat your bread with enjoyment, and drink your wine with a merry heart; for God has already approved what you do" (Eccl. 9:7).

A fruitful harvest, including good wine, was promised by God if the people were faithful and obedient (Deut. 7:12–13; 11:13–14).

John the Baptist, a Nazarite from birth, was committed to a very strict diet and abstained from wine drinking. When Jesus began his ministry, he mixed with people and joined them at parties. His critics leveled severe charges against him. To those charges Jesus replied: "For John came neither eating nor drinking, and they say, 'He has a demon'; the Son of man came eating and drinking, and they say, 'Behold, a glutton and a drunkard, a friend of tax collectors and sinners!' " (Matt. 11:18–19).

While it is certain that Jesus was falsely accused of gluttony and drunkenness, he did admit to eating and drinking with people.

John records Jesus' first miracle. It was at a wedding feast at which the host ran out of wine (John 2:1–11). At the request of his mother, Jesus turned water into wine. According to the testimony of the steward of the feast, the wine Jesus made was the best served during the day. The effect of the miracle of turning water into wine? "This, the first of his signs, Jesus did at Cana in Galilee, and manifested his glory; and his disciples believed in him."

Paul prohibits drunkenness on the part of bishops and deacons in 1 Timothy 3. However, he simply says of deacons that they must be "not addicted to much wine" (v. 8).

And what person proposing total abstinence has not been challenged by the opposition's quoting of Paul's advice to Timothy? "No longer drink only water, but use a little wine for the sake of your stomach and your frequent ailments" (1 Tim. 5:23).

In the three passages just cited, the Greek word used for wine is *oinos*. The word normally refers to fermented juice of the grape. The Greek word for unfermented grape juice is *troox.*

Some have argued that the wine in biblical days was not intoxicating, or at least not as much as present-day alcoholic beverages. While it may be that today's brewing methods make stronger drinks, it is obvious that people in biblical days could get drunk on their wine.

Is there a biblical case for total abstinence? Legalistically, *no.* There simply is no commandment, "Thou shalt not drink." The Bible prohibits drunkenness, but wine was a part of the culture that was not directly opposed by Christ or biblical writers. Admission of this fact is simply the result of an honest evaluation of the biblical texts.

Yet, using biblical principles, today's Christian is led to total abstinence. That the Bible does not speak clearly against the use of alcohol should not lead to the conclusion that drinking is right. Many social wrongs existed in Jesus' day that he did not attack. Slavery is a prime example. His reason for coming to earth did not hinge on these issues, but rather on man's relationship to man and God. With divine intuition, he attacked those traditions that kept

God and man apart. By laying down basic principles, he provided guidelines for later generations of his followers to heal broken mankind.

The new case for total abstinence is based on biblical principles of concern for persons, and on modern knowledge of alcohol.

The Christian should refrain from drinking alcoholic beverages out of stewardship for his personal health.

The biblical principle is: "Do you not know that your body is a temple of the Holy Spirit within you, which you have from God? You are not your own; you were bought with a price. So glorify God in your body" (1 Cor. 6:19–20).

This is a fact of modern medicine: The liver, heart, and brain all are affected by alcohol. Even a moderate drinker loses some brain cells every time he drinks. Brain cells are irreplaceable. They die because alcohol chokes off the oxygen supply to the cells.

Another biblical principle is concern for the welfare of others. Jesus said, "You shall love your neighbor as yourself."

In 1968, 55,500 people lost their lives in highway accidents. Half of those were killed in alcohol-related accidents, according to J. Marse Grant, in *Whiskey at the Wheel* (Broadman, 1970).

Grant goes on to answer the challenge: "Surely, a moderate drinker is not dangerous." The American Insurance Association says that after only one or two drinks the critical judgment of a driver and his ability to react quickly in an emergency are seriously impaired.

Christians in biblical times did not face the social conditions of our day. They did not drink and then drive powerful automobiles on crowded streets.

One of the principal arguments of the drug user in his fight for legalization of drugs is that alcohol is more harmful than drugs. Medical authorities insist that marijuana is less harmful than beer. Alcohol, then, has no more place in society than dangerous drugs. Which would show the more concern for a neighbor: the moderate drinker or the total abstainer?

The Christian is freed from legalism. He is not, however, free from his own conscience nor may he use his freedom to hurt others.

Paul used the case of eating certain foods and of drinking wine as a point of Christian freedom. He stated: "I know and am persuaded in the Lord Jesus that nothing is unclean in itself" (Rom. 14:14). However, if someone is hurt by the Christian's use of alcohol, then the Christian—even though he is not convicted of its wrong—should abstain.

Paul's principle is, "Do not, for the sake of food, destroy the work of God. Everything is indeed clean, but it is wrong for any one to make others fall by what he eats; it is right not to eat meat or drink wine or do anything that makes your brother stumble" (Rom. 14:20–21).

The most prized possession of a Christian is his influence. Because alcohol has caused so much harm and tragedy, it is looked upon as an inherent evil by many people—including many who drink. For the Christian to drink means he would lose his influence and witness. No drink is worth that.

The Christian does not stand so much *against* "demon alcohol" as he stands *for* people. When he reviews the readily available statistics on broken homes, crime, accidents, and wasted lives, he concludes that alcohol—like drugs—is a commodity that deteriorates society. The challenge that alcoholism is only a symptom of deeper distress compels the Christian to seek deeper solutions. But he is convinced that drinking is more than an outgrowth; that it creates its own set of problems, too.

The new case for an old conviction is simply that the Christian abstains from alcoholic beverage out of his concern for persons, including himself. In retrospect, maybe Billy Sunday's words were not too strong after all.

---

[1] William T. Ellis, *"Billy Sunday," the Man and His Message* (Philadelphia: The John C. Winston Co., 1914), p. 97.

[2] All Scripture passages in this chapter are from the Revised Standard Version.